SLIPSTREAM

Catherine Cole is an Australian-British writer who currently lives in Liverpool, where she is a Professor of Creative Writing and a member of some of the city's key cultural committees.

Her publications include four acclaimed novels, a short story collection, a memoir, and an academic monograph on crime fiction. She has also edited two anthologies, one on fashion in fiction and the other on Vietnamese writers and writing.

Slipstream

on Memory
and Migration

CATHERINE COLE

Valley Press

First published in 2023 by Valley Press
Woodend, The Crescent, Scarborough, YO11 2PW
www.valleypressuk.com

ISBN 978-1-915606-34-1
Cat. no. VP0227

Cover photograph by Jason Patrick Schuller.
Cover and text design by Jamie McGarry.

Printed and bound in Great Britain by
Imprint Digital, Upton Pyne, Exeter.

Contents

This book is dedicated to the memory of my brother,

Brian Cole,

who died in April 2022.

Family narrative and social narrative are one and the same.

Annie Ernaux

Beyond myself, somewhere, I wait for my arrival.

Octavio Paz

Your nostalgia has created a non-existent country, with laws alien to earth and man.

Georgious Seferis

Introduction

On a long-haul flight between Australia and the UK, I pondered what it means to be a migrant. Flying often makes me anxious and introspective, and my thoughts fluttered between the little screen on which an unmemorable film was playing, and the seat belt sign that pinged occasionally when the plane met turbulence. I felt adrift, weary, not just of the journey but also of my role as a commuter between two continents, migrating away from my friends and family in Sydney and towards my ambition to experience life as an academic in England.

For the past decade, I seem to have been always on the move, driven by the desire to be in new places where something exciting awaited. The essayist, James Wood, talks of this peripatetic restlessness in his essay, 'On Not Going Home', as 'the familiar march of the provincial for the metropolis.' In my case, this march involved more than just my academic ambition. It also was that of a migrants' child ambitious to know more of her 'home' country, England, which my parents left in 1949.

Through our departures, Wood argues, these 'authentic and oddly artificial' journeys, we experience an 'exodus of expansion.' Not much felt expansive during my cramped and tedious flight; just a hollow sense of inevitable loss, of things being given up. There was anxiety in my ruminations too, and echoes of all the millions of people who left home, by choice or force, to go to another country: Why am I doing this? Why can't I just stay put and be happy with the life I have? Yet here I was doing it too. Travelling. Migrating.

Paramount amongst my anxious questioning was the sense that I had been infected in some way by a blight common amongst the children of migrants; that desire to experience a life missed in the country abandoned by my parents. Whatever the reasons, I felt misdirected, and un-qualified for what lay ahead.

James Wood explores this sense of an accidental life in 'On Not Leaving Home' too, identifying how easy it is for monumental journeys to be undertaken without much thought of consequence. 'What is peculiar, even a little bit-ter, about living for so many years away from the country of my birth,' Woods says:

> is the slow revelation that I made a large choice a long time ago that did not resemble a large choice at the time; that it has taken years for me to see this; and that this process of retrospective comprehension in fact constitutes a life – is indeed how life is lived. To think about home and departure from home, about not going home, and no longer feeling able to go home, is to be filled with a remarkable sense of (Freud's) 'afterwardness': it is too late to do anything about it now, and too late to know what should have been done.

As my journey progressed, the lens through which I was examining my family history became clouded with com-plexity. Was I keen to work in England because that was where I felt I really belonged? Was I curious about the country my parents had left? How much would growing up in Australia affect the ways in which I was accepted by col-leagues or students? What national qualities might I need to moderate in a country where class and accent were indel-ible social markers? These questions were not unique. The children of migrants often ask themselves who they are and how their family washed up on new shores. I certainly had, all my life. On the one hand, I had always felt Australian, on the other, English. There was no escaping this perplexing self-inquiry. It was a natural by-product of a life lived between two cultures – my own and my parents'. In the end, I had discovered, you feel oddly out of place in both.

My identity is that of a first-generation child in a new country. Born into it, becoming of it. That is my Australian identity and I cheerfully claim it. The other is the country gifted by my parents – that England, that Yorkshire of lore and memories and family. My Yorkshire identity slips and spins; a story shared but not lived. I have no doubt that this complex duality of the real and the imagined countries contributed to the writer I became. All those stories and photographs and parcels from relatives in England had cultivated my imagination. I could exercise my own creative impulses as a child by imagining myself in my parents' former lives. My creative landscape germinated in their stories of Yorkshire's pits and industrial towns, of dales and beach outings, and so I began to write.

Australia's history is embroidered with meditations such as these, of families who migrated and lived to regret it or soldiered on, determined to make a better home on alien shores, or those who thought they'd just experience the country for a while but soon found themselves emotionally tied to their new home. In his book, *The Old Greeks*, the Greek-Cypriot writer, George Kouvaros, reflects upon these accidental choices as '…the question that shadows so many tales of migration.' Migrants 'faced with the impossibility of retracing time' return to the places they left, 'searching for memories that branch off in multiple directions like cracks on a concrete floor.' We daydream, Kouvaros says, 'about things that may or may not have happened.' When I read Kouvaros' words, I decided those cracks on the floor represented my family; my barely-known cousins and aunts and grandparents given up to parcels, photographs, letters, to being experienced through the murmurs and mediations of distance.

I stopped over in Hong Kong for a few days to break my long journey, and while there my thoughts continued to play with ideas of migration. The reverie on belonging that had overtaken me on the plane consumed me again while I was sitting on a bus in Hong Kong's Central District. My explorations of Hong Kong had become oppressively singular; I watched other people, in couples and in groups, laughing and sharing stories or pointing things out to one another. The city teemed with families who seemed welded to their lives there. They went back a long way, I decided, generations and generations, or so it seemed to me on that humid, solitary day. For decades, Hong Kong has been home to refugee camps and resettlement schemes to address the political and social turmoil in the region, from the Vietnamese fleeing the communist victory in their country in 1975 to incoming migrants and guest workers from China and the Philippines. They form their own national networks, such as the Filipino housemaids you see in happy chattering groups every Sunday, enjoying a day off with their compatriots.

A little while later, a glimpse of water – a bay, with an island rising from the richly turquoise sea – reminded me of Sydney's Eastern suburbs in the way that Sydney so often nonchalantly draws you to her wherever you are in the world. I could think of nothing but picnics in the bush, ferry rides to Manly Beach or barbecues in backyards shaded by giant gum trees.

Simone Weil said that to be rooted is perhaps the most important and least recognised need of the human soul. Am I homesick, I wondered, uprooted, as I made my way towards Hong Kong's Stanley Market, or am I just recalibrating myself for the life I'll pick up again in the UK? I decided I was mourning what I was leaving in Sydney, before letting it go.

It's easy to ruminate like this when you're in transit. You're caught in the chasm between here and there, departure and welcome, one home and another. Home takes on a form of romanticism because you've lost your hold on it. It taunts you because suddenly a real home, one organically rooted in your past, no longer seems achievable. This should not have been surprising to me. Home had become a fluid concept during the past decade. I commuted between Sydney and Melbourne for three years while I worked at a university in Melbourne. I commuted between Sydney and Wollongong on the New South Wales coast for a further seven years, staying down the coast most weeknights because I was too tired at the end of each day to face the long drive home through the Royal National Park or along the highway. This reflective pause between places taught me a number of things: the importance of family, the way commuting sheds friends too easily, how a home slips away like a carelessly moored ship, and how easy it is to confuse where you are with where you really want to be. Commuting between Sydney and Liverpool in the UK, taking advantage of points of transfer such as Hong Kong to break a long flight, was surely an inevitable next stage of this peripatetic life. In a place like Hong Kong, I could try to defy jetlag while listening to the wing beat of my Australian self, left to make its return flight to Sydney alone.

In Hong Kong I recognized, too, that I am one of the

fortunate generations for whom freedom of movement has been a right and a privilege. My parents' migration to Australia just after the Second World War bestowed on me a UK passport and the freedom to live and work as a British/Australian citizen in Europe, at least until Brexit took away that right. For a more prosperous life in Sydney for their kids, my parents sacrificed their families and friends in Yorkshire, their sense of who they were and their generational histories. They were not alone in this desire for a better life, a desire that continues to animate migrants and refugees all over the world – and which will gain an even greater imperative as pandemics and climate change play havoc with already-fragile lands.

My parents' journey in 1949 formed part of one of the world's largest mass migrations. In the seventy-two years since their departure from England, some 240 million migrants have moved abroad in search of jobs, better education and health services, while another 740 million people have migrated internally for the same reasons. When refugees are added to that figure, one billion out of eight billion people in the world today are refugees or migrants; or in other words, one in seven of us has made a new home somewhere on the globe. Why then, are we so unsympathetic to those who need a safe place? When watching as people flee wars, march towards closed borders or apply fruitlessly for economic migration, it is easy to forget just how fortunate our own families were.

I made the long haul back to Liverpool, one of the UK's most culturally vibrant cities, with its uncertain weather, poverty and high unemployment – all those social evils my parents migrated to Australia to escape. Where, I asked myself again, was the social glue I had longed for in Hong

Kong, the extended family and networks of friends I had built throughout my lifetime? Where was my true home and why had I moved again? I wondered how I might reflect on and write about the ways in which my privilege might be compared, with empathy and activism, to the lives of people struggling to achieve what my parents were able to access – migration. We migrants share stories of uprooting, loss and struggle, yet we fail to reflect sympathetically on those in need of similar opportunities. Why was this?

In response to these questions, I decided to write this story about my first 'home', the life in the north of England abandoned by my parents. I would explore why the pull of that past life, lived by my family before I was born and through their memories and stories throughout my childhood, had asserted itself so potently in Hong Kong. Why had I chosen to move between countries to live and work in Britain when I had a perfectly lovely home in Sydney? Liverpool isn't even in Yorkshire but the neighbouring 'enemy' county of Lancashire, as I joked with friends before I left Sydney. The rivalry between the two counties goes back further than the Wars of the Roses, and is as much about culture and place as tales of warring barons. I could even remember my mother referring to it when I was little; she was insulted if anyone mistook her Yorkshire accent for a Lancashire one. Yet here I was, an Aussie in Liverpool, working, writing and thinking about the ironies and incongruities of reverse migration.

Being Australian in Liverpool has its advantages as well as pitfalls. 'Scousers', as the locals are informally known, invariably have a friend or family member in Australia, or they have visited the country themselves at some point and have fond memories of beaches and sun. We talk about their relatives in Brisbane, Sydney, Adelaide, about the heat or the great distance between our two countries, the conversation invariably ending in a question of why I left Sydney to live in the north of England. 'I love your city,' I respond. 'I love the culture. I want to get to know all things English better, especially the England my parents might have experienced had they stayed.' 'I'm here for work,' I sometimes add, as a kind of professional addendum, though I suspect my academic career may not have unfolded in quite the same way had my working-class parents not decided to leave the UK.

That decision, so privileged in the context of the physical and political barriers that have closed off so many borders today, was made in the late 1940s by two people who had never even ventured as far south as London, and it rests at the heart of this story. It led to the emigrant child's inevitable question – what would my life have been like had my family stayed put?

As I viewed – with some jealousy – the Hong Kong families during my journey's transit stop, I asked myself what I might have shared with dozens of uncles and aunts and cousins in Yorkshire if my parents had remained at home. These questions are impossible to answer, of course. My parents left, and nothing can reverse that decision, but it is hard to avoid the ways in which this 'what-if' probing becomes an itch. Memories, especially the ones borrowed from parental reveries and family stories, need to be re-evaluated to weigh their true worth. How much of my family history was real, how much was nostalgic fabrication, and why did these accounts of an abandoned life shape my childhood imagination in the manner they did? How did those stories make me the writer I became, despite my rare attempts to capture any of them in the novels or short stories I've written so far?

'One key theme to emerge in oral histories of migration is the cross-generational possibilities for remembering and forgetting,' write Kate Darian-Smith and Paula Hamilton in their essay collection, *Remembering Migration: Oral Histories and Heritage in Australia.* In the chapters that follow, I reflect on my family's migration and our cross-generational attempts to understand it. Each chapter offers an examination of the impact of my parents' decision on our lives, most notably on our sense of identity and the characters we wove from it – ourselves.

In particular, I wanted to address our conundrums, to discover something new about the world my parents left on the migrant ship, the *Empire Brent*, and the UK I re-entered in 2017; to capture something of that family story, a history common to the millions of migrants who have settled in Australia, but also the history unique to my family. In the process I hope to become what George Gusdorf has called 'the writer who remembers and wants to gain acceptance for this or that revised and corrected version' of their past, their private reality. Stories about migration offer empathy, I would argue, and we certainly need personal and societal empathy to care for and support today's migrants and refugees; to understand why so many people have been forced to flee their homes. We also need to remember: once, that was me.

Throughout their lives, my parents remained proudly British, part of a hegemonic, colonial culture that asserted itself in numerous social, cultural and political ways to affirm they belonged in Australia by historical birthright. British they may have been, but their Yorkshireness was another matter altogether. It labelled them as regional, *northern* English and it was through this identity that they displayed their eccentricities and differences. Despite these geographical markers of place, class and background, they shared many common experiences with migrants of non-English speaking backgrounds who settled in Australia, from Northern, Eastern and Southern Europe, the Middle East and Southeast Asia – all striving as my parents did, to make a new home while retaining their memories about and connections to their old one.

Like so many children of migrants who create a richly-detailed narrative of the past, I also want to revisit my parents' old 'stomping grounds' to talk to the ghosts who populate their former lives. What might I gain from these encounters? Self-understanding, historical context, peace of mind in regards to my oddly misshapen identity, that layered self I carry about with me; Australian, British, global, one of the 'citizens of everywhere and nowhere,' as described by the former UK Prime Minister, Teresa May?

'My mission (is) to irrigate the present with hope,' wrote the Palestinian author, Atef Abu Saif. 'I write to keep the life of this family moving forward.' I know I'm moving forward in search of a home, and I suspect I will only find it when I know the places my parents knew and recalibrate some of their stories in the context of today's Britain, but I'm also looking for the kind of English home I'd have lived in had my parents stayed in Yorkshire. To do this, I am embarking on a journey through Yorkshire with the ghosts of my family, following them north across Lancashire and Cumberland to their stepping off point on the Clydeside docks of Glasgow. What did they jettison in that fateful embarkation and what travelled with them over the seas? I want to recreate the ways in which Yorkshire and the North of England migrated with my family to the Southern Hemisphere, to Sydney's southwestern suburbs and the home my parents built in Bankstown. I want to chronicle how they plaintively memorialised the old world while staying ambitious and optimistic for the new one.

This book was also written in gratitude for my parents' two specific forms of sacrifice. The first was for their storytelling, those sometimes-painful yarns which spoke of loss and regret, of humour and laughter and all the details about beloved places that found their way into my own imaginings later on. The second was their journey away from their country to give their children a better life in a new one. From this I learned that determination is needed to make 'a go of' the new land, and that migration requires courage and tenacity. My family could have gone back to Yorkshire, but they didn't. They stuck it out through those particularly tough post-war years, and the whole family was rewarded by their decision. Such are the gifts that migrants give their children.

CHAPTER ONE
The Sea

My brother doesn't remember much of our family's departure from the United Kingdom on the *Empire Brent*. He was five years old at the time and my sister had just turned three. There were farewells and packing and decisions about which toys to keep and which to give away. Not the Hornby train set we fought over years later, thank goodness, that cardboard box full of perfect little replica steam trains, tracks and tiny people, miniature milk cans, and tin platforms with tin stations painted to look like brick. The family possessions were packed into a motley assortment of trunks – some leather, some wicker – and wooden crates, all carefully marked for the hold. Personal luggage for the six-week voyage was limited to a few pieces of cabin baggage only, so weather-appropriate clothes were anticipated for a sea journey that would take the family from Glasgow, along the west coast of the UK and France. Past Gibraltar. Through the Suez Canal. Down the long stretch of the Indian Ocean from Aden to Fremantle, my family's first Australian landfall.

Sometime before this, my parents had visited a Commonwealth Office in the north of England to apply for an assisted passage. Husband, wife, two small children. They had the advantage of cousins in Sydney who would sponsor them and organise a place to stay until work was found. They must have announced their intentions to brothers and sisters – nine on my mother's side and three on my father's, all of them living close by in that part of South Yorkshire bounded by Barnsley, Wakefield and Sheffield. My father worked at Royston's Monkton Pit – not underground, that was always an important clarification, but as a foreman plate layer. He'd started straight from school as a labourer on the pit railway and had worked his way up to foreman through ganger and fettler jobs. Other members of his family worked at Monkton Pit too, some over-ground, some under, and any discussion about the pit and its workings invariably contained stories of the lives of coal miners such as my grandfather; rather wistful ones it seemed to me, as though the blackened pit workers belonged to a more romantic branch of the family.

The years just after the Second World War hadn't been kind to the UK. The weather conspired with rationing and bomb damage to create a bleak return to peace. In the winter of 1947 snow fell somewhere in Britain for fifty-five days straight and the north of England experienced its worst weather conditions in thirty years. So thick was the snow that people in the nearby Dales remained buried in their houses, managing as best they could until someone dug them out. Food rationing meant provisions were restricted, so constructing family meals required long queues. I thought it all sounded rather exciting when, as a child, I first heard these stories of privation and icy-cold landscapes. By then I had been introduced to the world of British storytellers like Enid Blyton and Noel Streatfield, who made the Second World War sound such great fun in books like *The Adventurous Four* and *The Children of Primrose Lane*.

My father's mother had just died and the bonds that tied him to place had loosened. This wasn't helped by some kind of family nastiness about who should get her possessions. All this set my family on its journey.

If we are to understand the outlook that drove migrants like my parents to leave, 'we need to look beyond the well-known hardships, to the pervasive psychology of gloom which gripped so much of post-war Britain.' For many people this 'persisted well past the worst years of austerity,' write Hammerton and Thomson in their comprehensive study of post-war British migration, *Ten Pound Poms: Australia's Invisible Migrants*. 'In so many migrant stories,' they argue, 'this sense of post-war despair is contrasted with later good fortune in Australia, in a vindication of the decision to emigrate.'

The weather and the pervasive gloom in the post-war north of England certainly played a key role in my parents' departure, and I like to think it galvanized them into an impulsive sense of adventure, however briefly ignited. My mother rarely said anything about what made her decide to leave, but something certainly pushed her into the plan. Perhaps the force of my father's will propelled them, or perhaps a desire to escape Yorkshire's soot-blackened back-to-backs, the pit whistles calling a start or an end to a shift, and the ration queues. Whatever her reason, my mother said very little about what she'd have preferred. A decision was made. They were going.

When I first visited England in the 1970s I was shocked by what I found. I hadn't at that stage fallen in love with Sydney's inner-city terraced houses, so the smoke-stained and tiny places I encountered, first in London and then in Yorkshire, seemed far too small and mean. Some of my aunts and uncles still didn't have a proper bathroom and if I wanted a bath I needed to request one a few days out. That way a fire could be lit and the boiler behind the fireplace heated up, and the bath with its wooden flap-cover in the kitchen could be cleared of kitchen utensils, cleaned and filled. For the rest of the time I was expected to make do with a good scrub at the kitchen sink with a sponge and cake of soap.

I too was a sponge that first visit, absorbing all the sounds and smells that felt so familiar, so pre-lived, that I began to wonder if they had been passed on genetically. They included the pervasive scent of coal fires that rose from domestic chimneys, the coal tar and sulphurous smell of Monkton's coke ovens. I loved the sticky pink sweetness of the corner sweetshop, with its jars of bulls' eyes and fruit pastilles, and the Pomfret cakes that my father talked about wistfully all his life with boyish greed. I watched the cigarette smoke of the local pub curl towards the ceramic beer pulls, and men in tweed flat caps who silently looked me up and down before returning to talk of the latest Leeds United victory. It was exotic yet familiar. I could have lived there all my life, but I also felt alien; too robustly Australian and curious, in an era when a young woman's place in a pub was at a table with her girlfriends and a little bottle of Babycham.

Packing done, trunks sent ahead, unwanted furniture, clothes and toys dispersed to siblings, my family took a train from Wakefield to Manchester, then north to Glasgow. My brother remembers very little of that leg of the voyage. It was his first train journey through alien territory and whenever I cross the Pennines these days, I see his boy-ghost glued to the train window, watching the ragged peaks outside. Did he pass through Slaithwaite and Marsden? See the Calder Valley scattered with the stone warehouses and mills famous for their weaving? At some point, the family changed trains in Manchester or Preston, lugging suitcases and bags up and down station stairs, my father no doubt manifesting the anxiety about missed trains that dogged him all his life. Then on they went to Glasgow, where they caught a rickety bus to a Clyde-side wharf. There, the *Empire Brent* was moored.

There is something special about embarking on a sea voyage that air travel can never match. A ship waiting at a dock, its engines pulsing, is a living thing. It carries a miasma, a veneer of all the memories of previous sea voyages, layers of salt and fuel, meals and luggage and people. Ships carry what Gillian Whitlock describes as 'the weight of maritime histories and migrations that percolate through living memory.' In *Down to the Sea in Ships,* the British writer, Horatio Clare, suggests this atmosphere 'is as though ships have spirits, good or ill, which are not merely the sum of their histories and the personalities of their crews.' The passengers on the *Empire Brent* would have felt this history settle on them as soon as they embarked, the ship's past sea stories whispering in their ears.

As they entered the first of the *Empire Brent's* labyrinthine corridors the passengers were segregated, men and boys to one deck, women and children to another. The ship was due to sail on Wednesday, 13 July, 1949, but superstition about the date meant that she stayed tethered to her Clyde-side mooring till one minute past midnight, Thursday, 14 July. Who knows what sea monsters the *Empire Brent* would have encountered had she sailed on the 13th? Unluckily for the captain, for whom this was the last voyage before retirement, he would die and be buried at sea in the Indian Ocean somewhere between Aden and Fremantle. My brother still clearly remembers the Captain's canvas-wrapped body being jettisoned from the deck, the ship's chaplain offering prayers at sea while the passengers looked on with a mix of horror, bemusement or anxiety as his body disappeared beneath the water.

Their sea voyage coloured my parents' new lives with a potent mix of wonder, nostalgia, and a certain disbelief that the 12,000 miles between Glasgow and Sydney could be covered in a ship. It was unimaginable for people who had never been on any kind of boat or ferry before, the children of pit workers who'd grown up in the social confines of Royston; the journey was as exciting as it was terrifying, and their thoughts dwelled on all they had left behind. The sea stories they recounted after the trip pulsed with anxiety and the pain of their loss. 'Migration is not just about a dispersal of individuals across continents; it is about a dispersal of the narrative details that we use to understand the people close to us,' wrote George Kouvaros of his own family's exodus.

As my parents travelled, their future narratives took shape, and in their voyage rested the seeds of generations of family stories, all of them interlacing humour and pathos. I can still hear these stories, told in my father's strong Yorkshire accent, the smells and sounds and adventures of a boyhood in Yorkshire enhanced with the salt and sea and waves of his voyage away from his history. Those narrative details became a memory map of Yorkshire superimposed on Sydney, and as I walked around my parents' old stomping grounds in Royston during that first visit to England, I couldn't help wondering how they'd done it, how they'd just upped and left. All my life they had been cautious, unadventurous people. How had they pulled together the courage to leave behind this close-knit, northern community? It takes a lot of guts to do it even now, but back then, when they'd just survived the horrors of the Second World War, their decision seemed particularly brave. I've travelled to far more places than my parents ever did, some requiring stamina or courage, some off the beaten tracks of tourism; yet none of my trips seems to hold within it the sheer audacity of the post-war, mass migration of which they were a small part. Need drove people, as did the pull of escape – optimism too, but this was also helped by a heady recklessness, a desire to build a new life a long way from the post-war ruin that had become so oppressive to them.

The cost of decisions such as theirs is often measured in pain. Atef Abu Saif grew up in Jaffa, listening to stories of one of Palestine's most vivid cities. 'I always had the impression,' he wrote:

> that the tellers of these stories were in actual, physical pain as they narrated; I imagined them with some covered wound, which quietly bled as they spoke. It was not that they were still living in the past, nor that the past haunted them. It was that they had been abandoned by the past. They had lost it somehow, and needed to reassure themselves that it had ever happened at all.

I would like to ask my father, dead more than thirty years now, why he remained so anxious, so 'in pain', all his life. Anxiety travels with you and from all accounts he'd been an anxious child, the last one, the 'change of life' baby, conceived when his mother thought her reproductive capacity was spent. She was overprotective of him, his older brothers told me. She turned him into a 'sugar baby', a description that coloured my imagining of him when I was a child. He was someone so petted he might melt away, dissolve; molten and crumbled like a sweet on the end of a tongue. His mother had also infected him with her own anxieties; her fear of doctors and the local infirmary, and of getting lost or straying too far from home. I suspect the answer to my question about his constant anxiety rests in his 'covered wounds' too. His decision to migrate exacerbated his fears: it made him guilty of the crime of inflicting pain on others.

He was responsible for what the family lost as well as what they gained from migration.

Yet my father boarded a migrant ship, his wife and two young children in tow. His mother's hold on him had loosened with her death, as had his ties to place. The Yorkshire he wrote about, however briefly, in his ill-kept and erratic diaries might document a Dales cycling trip or a film at the cinema in Barnsley one week, only to offer a gap as wide as Yorkshire itself before the next entry. At what point on his sea journey did he realise the monumentality of what he had done? Travelling through time zones, across the meridians and the equator, did he move, as Edward Said has suggested, to a different calendar, one that is 'less seasonal and settled than life at home'? Said believed exile to be de-centred and contrapuntal. I suspect my father's counterpoint involved a tethering to the anxieties that trapped him. He was forever caught between his indulged and frightened childhood and the over-responsibility and guilt of the husband and parent who has driven his family to abandon their old home for a new one on the other side of the world.

Loss was paramount to my mother's personality too. She left behind a mother with whom she was very close. Her father was a difficult man, a bully, by all accounts, who had been scarred as a child from his own father's abuse. There had been three sisters, six brothers; though her older sister, Theresa, and youngest brother, Ralph, had died before my mother left the UK of TB and diphtheria respectively. Where are they buried? I have no idea. The dead played no great role in our family narratives in Australia. I always suspected that the relatives my parents left behind just waved them off and got on with things, resuming their Yorkshire lives, the gap created by my family's departure quickly closing over as does water. The loss of family for my mother remained acute. This was given full voice in 1963 when my grandmother – by then free to travel after my grandfather's death in 1956 – arrived in Sydney on the P&O liner, *Himalaya*. As she spied her mother at the ship's rail my mother gave the sort of shriek I equate with an animal caught in a predator's jaws. Fourteen years of longing were released in that painful cry.

As I grew up, anxiety and loss such as my parents' seemed the legitimate state of the migrant. Most of my friends were the children of migrants too, so I often witnessed in their parents the same ruminating moodiness I saw in my father. My friends' parents overcame their fears in different ways. They drove cars while my father wouldn't, manufactured alcohol to drink in jollity – slivovitz or rough red wine pressed from the grape vines that festooned the homes of my Greek, Italian, Yugoslav and Lithuanian friends. They participated in cultural groups, their children decked in the embroidered and beribboned folk costumes of Eastern Europe, cooked food that tasted of former village ovens, turned their gardens into farmlets to provide for the fruit shops they ran. Yet beneath all that bonhomie and cultural clutching there remained a seam of fear. What I saw in my father I often saw in other parents too: a swift and startling recollection, like a bullet, a sudden anxious awareness that they had travelled a long way from home.

The Australian cultural historian, Ghasan Haghe, cautions against seeing this migrant sadness as a negative thing and suggests making a clear distinction between diasporic memory and homesickness. Homesickness, Haghe argues:

> is, as its name suggests, a sickness: a state where one's memory of back home plays a debilitating function and produces a state of passivity, where the subject is unable to

"deploy" himself or herself in the environment in which he or she is operating. This is why nostalgia should not be conceptually collapsed with homesickness, as it can readily be conceived in a far more positive light as an enabling memory. Far too often, the collapsing of all migrant yearning for home into a single "painful" sentiment is guided by a "miserabilist" tendency in the study of migration that wants to make migrants passive pained people at all costs.

The children of migrants are acute observers of homesickness and puzzle at the ways in which it infects family life. In the midst of my parents' fear and sacrifice, I often found myself asking whether migration really offered the freedom and scope that families like ours pursued, relocating themselves as they had to the other side of the world at a time when return or regular family contact was limited. Were my parents exiles or had they just swapped one place for another, fleeing nothing other than post-war privation, their lives and lands never in danger? For Edward Said, exile 'is strangely compelling to think about but terrible to experience.' It is:

the unhealable rift forced between a human being and a native place, between the self and its true home: its essential sadness can never be surmounted. And while it is true that literature and history contain heroic, romantic, glorious, even triumphant episodes in an exile's life, these are no more than efforts meant to overcome the crippling sorrow of estrangement. The achievements of exile are permanently undermined by the loss of something left behind forever.

When I first read Said's words as a university student, I

puzzled over the differences between voluntary migration and exile. My parents certainly acted like exiles even though they had chosen to leave England, and the family was soon well and truly settled in Australia. What then, is the difference between a place of involuntary exile and a chosen home? Drawing on her own experiences as a migrant, Susannah Radstone argues that no matter the differences between the two, migrants still feel lost and off-course. 'The position of a voluntary migrant permits no comparison with the rigours of those forced to leave their homes and loved ones,' she writes. 'Permitted or prescribed, even – however, by my position as a voluntary migrant and memory researcher, is an enquiry into memory's relations with that unsettling fusion of actual and psychical "off-courseness" that has accompanied my own migration.'

Radstone's 'off-courseness' offers insights into just how exiled a voluntary migrant can feel. The word *exile* carries with it the forced separation from a beloved place, a banishment with no hope of return. We read about the Roman Emperor Augustus' banishment of his daughter Julia to Pandataria, or Napoleon on Elba, or refugees from Palestine or Syria. Britain's unwanted convicts were exiled to Australia. Australian Aborigines were exiled from their lands. 'Off-courseness' suggests a sense of being lost or cast adrift in an unknown place. Given its history as a former British prison and colony, Australia sometimes seems to minimize the waves of migrants who have arrived since 1788 by force or circumstances, regretfully, fearfully, happily, but exiled prior to mass communication or social media, and travelling in the knowledge that they might never go home again. Their lived experiences, their memories, were exiled in the new land too, reshaped into a broken narrative, one which veers away from 'the fleshy immediacy' of the present, becoming instead a narrative of distortion. Through this process, past lives were idealized or litanised to fit with the expectations and mantras of the new place. To this day, my country's ubiquitous question posed to visitors, 'How are you liking Australia?' requires an answer swathed in approval and optimism.

In the article 'My Grandmother's £10 exile returned to haunt me,' the Australian writer and academic, Stephanie Bishop, describes the painful homesickness of her grandmother. Bishop's own reverse migration when she moved to England to complete a PhD brought her closer to a grandmother who had spent her life in Australia resenting her move. This sense of exile and grief never left her. 'My grandmother,' Bishop wrote:

had never lived anywhere other than England and identified intensely with the landscape and its people. When they left, they had four young children, and my grandmother discovered she was pregnant with a fifth on the voyage. She did not want to move, and has resented this, to varying degrees, ever since. Growing up in Australia, what I heard again and again was my grandmother complaining about this ill-fated event. Her longing for England never lessened. I can't remember a time when I was in her company and she did not say something about the great pleasures and beauty of England and compare Australia unfavourably. Yet in our family it was part of our routine entertainment to quietly mock my grandmother's grief. All the while, my grandfather silently bore her criticism, aware that his wife thought he had done her some great wrong. As a child, and young woman, I accepted the wider family's take: my grandmother was simply a whingeing pom.

Migration, I'd decided before I reached adulthood, is an existential plane, one in which the core of a person remains fixed in some way, forever cast into who you were when you lived in your former home. My parents certainly retained an 'otherness', a way of being that resisted the reshaping and reinvention that a new country offers. They were never really Australian; they were no longer English, so they held tight to that exiled inner self, the young man and woman who stepped onto the *Empire Brent* in Glasgow. How fearful it must have been to sense you might lose that part of yourself too; so known, so shaped, by generations in Royston.

Expectation had a lot to do with how a new identity might be forged. According to Hammerton and Thomson, migrants who were sponsored by relatives or friends in Australia were greatly influenced by their sponsors' portrayal of the country. And so it was with my family. After my father died, some answers offered themselves to my questions about his fears and how he overcame them to step aboard the *Empire Brent*. These were revealed when my mother gave my brother my father's green tin document box for safekeeping. My brother waited for years, not looking into it, until one day, he did. Inside he found ancient tax returns, pay slips, bills dating back to 1949 and two aerogrammes, one from my aunt and uncle in Sydney and dated 1947, extolling the good life in Australia. Their letter included a section written by one of their daughters, a young girl's description of Sydney's happy, relaxed lifestyle and what fun it was for children. The other was from Aunt Kate, my father's dearest relative in Barnsley, telling him to treat her £200 loan as a gift. These reassurances seemed to be precariously balanced with danger, a syren's call. Combined, they were as potent a casting off as Jason's or Ulysses' desire to set sail for different lands. A new beginning. Who could resist it? Tempered with this alloy of fear and hope, my family sailed away too.

Six weeks to Sydney. A long sea voyage develops its rhythms quickly. No sooner have the dockside gulls disappeared than the rituals begin. In calm waters, such as harbours and rivers, the ship moves purposefully towards her true partner, the sea. Then, at the conjunction of the waters, the ship begins to move differently. She rolls and pitches in these new currents. Anyone confident that they will never experience seasickness might think again at this point. Departing the UK, the voyage offered my parents a comfortable proximity to land for the first week of their voyage. So close to the coast were they, the sea birds came and went like visiting relatives.

Along to the Clyde mouth the *Empire Brent* sailed, past Greenock, into the Firth of Clyde and the Inner Sea. Travelling south in the Irish Sea, she passed close by the Isle of Man and Northern Ireland. Did my father stand on the deck hoping for a glimpse of the Mountains of Mourne, the subject of one of his favourite songs? Departing Glasgow at midnight must have meant these landmarks slipped by while the family was sleeping, but they may have watched as the ship sailed past Land's End, navigating towards the Cape of Saint Vincent on the southern tip of Portugal. As they saw the last of England, a clump of distant rocks on a milky horizon, did they share a mix of freedom, exhilaration and anxiety, with the sea heaving, the wind blustery, the clouds racing over them?

It is hard to describe the sea to people who have never been out on it. Not the polite sea of pleasure cruisers sliding across the glassy surface of a harbour, or the sheltered passage of a car ferry between islands. Not water taxis or yachts scudding between buoys. In the middle of the Indian Ocean, landfall a week in any direction, the sea becomes friend and enemy, someone you flatter or pay homage to, bribe, cajole, curse, congratulate. You learn why the ancient Greeks threw coins into the sea off Cape Sounion to appease their sea-god, Poseidon.

For my parents, England receded with each day at sea.

Yorkshire, Barnsley, Royston.

All gone.

Brothers and sisters, uncles and aunts, the lady who ran the dairy on the corner, the publican, the Barnsley Market stallholders.

All gone.

New passenger-friends were doing the same tie cutting. Shy ones, scared ones, men full of braggadocio and women, like my mother, silently weeping for their 'Mams'. There is a family story about the Yorkshire pit ponies who laboured underground alongside the miners, pulling carts full of freshly-harvested coal to where it would be loaded for transport above ground. These ponies would only go up on miners' picnic days, but when they were let loose in a field they displayed their ecstatic joy as they cantered around, neighing, shaking their manes, expanding themselves into the open air. I like to imagine this is what it felt like on that great field of Indian Ocean as my parents sailed towards Fremantle.

A sea passage is slow and reflective. A week to landfall, nothing to see but sea, nowhere to go but to sit by the rails watching the rise and fall, the water changing its mood to match the sky's, to succumb to the moon's tidal pull. My family huddled together on the upper deck, sometimes playing deck games with a ball that disappeared overboard in the rough waters of the Bay of Biscay – and into the archive of family sea stories that I could recite verbatim by the time I began school. My brother explored the lifeboats, to the chagrin of the ship's officers, and struck up a friendship with one of the radio operators on the Bridge. The family parted at night for their respective dormitories, my parents sleeping apart for the whole trip. There must have been days when they felt as free as those Yorkshire pit ponies, despite the gender-segregated dormitory cabins, the dull meals, seasickness, and the discombobulation of life without land. The sea offered its freedoms too, and so the family enjoyed them, on deck, standing at the prow, spying flying fish and porpoises – or so they thought, though they probably saw just frothy, playful waves painting sea memories for them.

Questions of migration, of the forfeited home country, drove my understanding of who I was and the culture I had come from. I decided the only answer was to go back to the source. To do so I too must travel by sea. My first sea voyage to the UK in the 1970s was taken on a Russian ship, the *Taras Shevshenko*, named after a Ukranian poet. I wasn't keen on flying and anyway, I wanted to experience a voyage like the one my family had talked so much about. I wasn't alone in my resolve. A sea voyage back to the 'mother country' was a rite of passage when I was a teenager and it had made its way into Australia's literary culture in books like Martin Boyd's *Lucinda Brayford*, Christina Stead's *For Love Alone* and Glenda Adams' *Dancing on Coral*. We wanted to head 'home' to the UK, to Europe, anywhere but the colonised place, that stolen indigenous Australia in which we found ourselves.

On the *Taras Schevshenko* I spent a leisurely five weeks travelling to the UK via New Zealand, Tahiti, the Panama Canal and the Dutch Antilles. It was a trip of sights and sensations, from Port Venus near Papeete in Tahiti, where I stood in the same spot as Captain Cook and Joseph Banks when they observed the transit of Venus in 1769. Or when I watched the Chilean sailing ship, the *Esmeralda*, a four-masted barquentine, being lowered behind us through the Panama Canal's various locks, her masts and rigging a spider's web against an enamel blue sky. Like me, the other young passengers were on their way to backpack around the UK and Europe. All of us were the children of migrants, drawn 'homeward' as salmon are to spawning grounds up-stream, children determined to experience for themselves what they had already lived through their parents' memories. We partied and drank and danced our way across the moonlit oceans, sailing closer and ever closer to our family histories.

For my parents the *Empire Brent* had been a far less luxurious ship. She began her maritime life in 1925 as the *SS Letitia* and she carried passengers until World War Two, predominantly between the UK and Canada. She was commissioned during the war as an armed troop carrier, her cabins stripped out to form dormitories for troops. When she was badly damaged in 1943, she stayed in Canadian waters as a hospital ship. She was purchased by the UK Ministry of Transport in 1946 and returned to civilian service, and *Letitia* was then renamed the *Empire Brent*. Unlike my ship, the *Empire Brent* boasted no library or indoor and outdoor swimming pools, bars and restaurants and floor-shows where the *Taras Schevshenko's* crew metamorphosed into balalaika playing singers or dancing troupes; but on the *Empire Brent* people sang and danced too, making their own entertainment. Families ate together at tables with sides that slid up to prevent their plates from crashing to the floor during rough weather. The food was post-war basic – soups and over-boiled meat and vegetables, custard and tinned fruit.

I made my parents' sea voyage in reverse on my second trip to the UK in the 1980s, again on a Russian ship, the *Shota Rustaveli* this time. She was named after a 12th century Georgian poet, again with a talented Soviet crew who washed the decks or served tables by day, only to appear at night to sing and dance us towards Southampton in shimmering costumes and floral, beribboned headdresses, or the pantaloons and astrakhan hats of Gogol's *Taras Bulba*. When we experienced a week of rough weather, much of it cyclonic, I too was inaugurated into how wide and treacherous the Indian Ocean can be. As the ship pitched and rolled, the elderly passengers were advised to stay in their cabins. Empty seasickness bags were placed strategically along the corridors for the more intrepid. I took myself onto the deck most days, springing as though on a trampoline each time the ship reared up against a wave.

It must have been hell to do the trip in a dormitory cabin shared with dozens of other passengers; women with children, men with boys. For almost a fortnight my mother was so seasick she was incapable of leaving her bunk and my father was frantic with worry. She emerged eventually, as skinny as a scarecrow. There is a photo of her on the *Empire Brent's* deck with my father and my brother. Both of them look fit and well, but my mother in her now-baggy suit, her face pinched behind her owl-round glasses, looks decidedly like she wishes she was back in Yorkshire.

When I began researching the *Empire Brent's* full history at the Mersey Maritime Museum in Liverpool, I hoped I might find a Liverpool connection. I wanted some association for her with my own new life in Liverpool, other than the now familiar one of troop carrier then migrant ship. I discovered that she'd been sold to the New Zealand government in the early 1950s to be renamed again, this time the *Captain Cook*. She was a more spruce ship as she plied New Zealand waters, and photos show her lounges looking smart in 1956, far more stylish than my family's memories of her. Eventually she was sold for scrap and returned to be broken up in Inverkeithing, Scotland, a stone's throw from where she'd begun her shipping life at Glasgow's Clyde dockyards in the nineteen-twenties, and my parents' stepping off point nearby.

Travelling by sea seems to open vast philosophical conundrums. It causes you to rethink your size and shape and mobility. It offers danger, beauty, secrets. You ponder them at dusk as the sun sinks into the ship's churning wake and syrens call you to them. Are you human? Your prehistory has returned your blood to the seawater from which your ancestors crawled. Questions pose themselves. Where exactly is Longfellow's secret of the sea, the heart of the great ocean? These oceanic rhythms and moods become biblical. Now you are in a close bond with the sea you might reconsider the meaning of 'deep calls to deep ... your waves and billows are gone over me' from the Old Testament's Psalm 42. Prayers. Poems. Snatches of music. This is how the sea calls to you.

Artists who have tried to capture the sea's heart have learned the challenges of painting water in motion. A landscape is fixed; it only moves with the passing of shadows and light, but the sea is in constant flux. It defies attempts to capture it, challenging seascape painters such as J.M. Turner, William Bond, John Constable and Samuel Walters who responded to its complexities by caging the sea within the parameters of their canvases. Despite their great skill, the artists' works remain just that – pictures of the sea. The sea seems to taunt their paint tubes – cobalt, cerulean, ultramarine, viridian, manganese blue, flake white, black – with her own permutations of sea-colour.

To be at sea is to give yourself over to all her tones and moods and movements. The sea heaves or shudders, rolls and rises – so do you. You respond to her commands. When she's rough, you endure. When calm, you marvel at how benign she can be. This conversation between ship and sea and passenger, between sea and shore, changes once you're through the Suez Canal, the Red Sea, the Gulf of Aden and into the Indian Ocean. Until now, the land has been comfortingly close but once Aden is behind you, there is no land, no landmark or point of reference. In the middle of a vast ocean, a sea voyage commands its own narrative. Its then that you wonder what would happen if the ship sank halfway between Aden and Fremantle. A week is a long time between ports, you realise. How long would it take a rescue ship to reach you?

I am sure sea rescues were on my father's mind all through the *Empire Brent's* passage. As soon as my family boarded her, they went through the shipwreck drill. In life jackets they stood by their designated lifeboat, visions of the *Titanic* awash in my father's imagination, I suspect; lifeboats lowering, the ship's orchestra bravely playing a hymn. There wouldn't have been a night when he didn't pray for the family's safe delivery to dry land, as nervous as were the sailors on Columbus' voyage, fearful of falling off the edge of the world.

My parents' life-long nostalgia for Yorkshire germinated from a seed planted as the *Empire Brent* was nudged away from her berth in Glasgow, and on and up it grew. It is an odd moment when ship and shore part – destabilizing and primal. Was it in that separation that they became what Ian Baucom describes as 'the backward-glancing English man or woman, domestic avatar of Walter Benjamin's Angel of History, turning a resentful back on the present and a teary eye toward the image of a vanishing England'?

My parents were not alone in their nostalgia. Between 1949 and 1975, subsequent generations of new Australians like them made their journeys from embarkation points in the UK and Europe. Just like my parents, most of these migrants were British, as Hammerton and Thomson note in *Ten Pound Poms*. Although large numbers of migrants came from other, non-English speaking countries throughout the 1950s and 1960s, 'the British comprised never less than a third and at times more than a half of all settler arrivals.'

Those British migrants travelled in ships like the *Strathnaver, Oronsay*, the *Oriana* and *Canberra,* far more luxurious vessels than those on which migrants who left immediately after the war travelled. Today, sites such as Facebook's 'Ten Pound Pom' group provide photos of families at dinner or by the pool, their children suntanned and happy, not quite believing their luck as they sail away from a tired old place to a better, newer one, or so they hoped. Their sea journey offered a break from reality – an isolated and unchallenged month in the middle of a vast expanse of water where the past and the future could be put on hold, worries forgotten, memories and homesickness stored away for a while. The energy and skills required to start again were recharged with sun, food, alcohol, sea games and rituals, like the crossing of the Equator when King Neptune came aboard to give his permission for the ship to cross the line between the Northern and Southern hemispheres.

In Hammerton and Thomson's *Ten Pound Poms,* the

English migrant, Sylvia Bannon, describes the pleasures of her voyage out in 1961, as the pilot ships led them into port:

> they would have streamers coming and they would have bands, you know, and music played ... And so everywhere we went it was like we were heralded ... and people would be there waving and it was exciting as anything ... the excitement of each port, and people being pleased to see us.

My own experience of these 'Ten Pound Pom' migrations came as I returned to Australia after my year of backpacking around Europe. I travelled home on the Chandris Line's *Australis*, a ship that paid scant attention to cleanliness, and passengers soon learned never to sunbathe down-wind of the funnel lest you found yourself covered in soot. On that voyage, *Australis* sailed from Southampton to Fremantle via Tenerife in the Canary Islands, then down the west coast of Africa to Cape Town, where I spent a day photographing apartheid's 'blacks only', 'whites only' signs in an impotent rage, my work in human rights advocacy in Australia still some years away. Most of the passengers on board the *Australis* were British and on an assisted passage. As the ship neared Fremantle, the sunbathing and partying over, the packing done, the sense of the passengers' apprehension became palpable and I remember thinking, 'this is what my parents must have felt.'

With their voyage soon to be over, the work of resettlement was about to begin. My parents' Yorkshire was gone and the herring gulls had long since flown back to their Clyde-side roostings. The sea continued to offer great open stretches of water but, as Australia drew ever closer, the sea also spoke more emphatically of the approaching new life in a new land. There was no escaping that responsibility and my father's anxieties would have grown with each sea mile. As the *Empire Brent* neared Fremantle, the new land with all its uncertainties and insecurities reached out to the passengers who stood on the decks looking for their first landmarks. They must have smelled soil, eucalyptus, the dusty dryness of ripening crops, the heady smells of shops and blossom and petrol as the vast Australian continent replaced the salt and the ozone and the oil of the ship's engines. What did the passengers feel as they realized that this was it: they were about to enter a new and unknown realm? All that was familiar, theirs, must now be recalibrated, changed.

When they finally reached Sydney my father's anxieties disembarked as eagerly as his nostalgia, travelling from Sydney's Pyrmont docks to my aunt's house in Bankstown, and taking residence there amongst the family's plans for a quarter acre block and a new fibrous cement house of their own. 'Fibro' they called it. Anxiety. My father was fearful of the steps he'd taken, of the new place and its new culture, of the cost of living and of building. As a result, the house only progressed as payments became available from his savings. It took almost five years to build and because he was worried he wouldn't earn enough as a civil servant, to cover costs he took a better-paid labouring job, a decision that still causes me heartache when I think how much cleaner and safer his working life would have been in an office. My distress is what George Kouvaros describes as 'the generational divide that took hold; the sad awareness of lives whose possibilities had been foreshortened by the demands of starting over.'

Was my father's life foreshortened?

Certainly.

I always felt his inner world was unexplored and unchallenged by migration too, yet when I asked him about it not long before he died, he deflected my concerns. What was the point of focusing on his own hopes, he indicated, in a myriad of ways. His migration, his sacrifice, had been made so his children and grandchildren could live better.

With our parents' deaths, Kouvaros argues:

the onus shifts to their children to gather together what remains and to account for what has been lost of these lives. How does one do this when the means by which a history is grasped is no more substantial than snatches of phrases, pieces of broken stories, and stubborn attachment to faded photographs?

There was no point in wondering needlessly about him and his potential, my father reiterated from his deathbed. He was happy and he wanted us to be happy too. Despite his reassurances, the onus that fell on me, I realized, was to backtrack and explore. To make my own story from their pre-story.

Perhaps this mix of reassurance and danger, born, surely, of the family's sea travel and their casting off, explains why arrivals and departures always have felt so profound for my family. My father repeatedly fretted and fussed before we left the house. He would check his pockets over and over again, go back to the toilet for a last nervous pee, make sure he'd locked the front door, that the gate was barred, that we were on time for the bus, that the bus would meet the train. There was the dash down the station steps in Bankstown to the platform and the hustle into the carriage, the thump of seats flipped to face one another. As the guard's whistle blew, we all gave a relieved sigh that we had made it. This moment was always transformative. We could sit back, look out the window, learn the names of the stations, reciting them until we knew the order perfectly.

The high school.

The Cook's River.

The Victorian shop facades, the wattle trees, the terrace houses.

All these denoted place more potently than name, so that a station became a Sunbeam iron advertisement or a giant plastic ice cream cone on the front of a shop, or a river whose *liet motif* was the sound of a train clattering over a railway bridge.

The sea stories would begin as soon as we entered Circular Quay; the Sydney Harbour Bridge an arched fretwork of iron, the harbour a dazzling blue. Oh, how seasick they were when the *Empire Brent* entered the Bay of Biscay. How lovely the Atlas Mountains looked with the sunset on them, the long turquoise strip of the Suez Canal, the date palms, the donkey carts, the camels visible from the ship's deck, Mount Sinai, the dhows off Aden. The stories continued as we made our way on the ferry to Manly Beach, across The Heads, the ferry rolling and tossing against the current. My younger sister and I were infected with the sea as surely as if we'd travelled from England on the *Empire Brent* with them. How inevitable it was then, that we'd both take whatever opportunity we could to travel by sea. We were just fulfilling our preordained sea destiny.

The sea in its various moods continued to shape my family throughout those early Australian years. We were drawn to it as though it offered a continuous migratory conversation, a link to the country and the people who had been left behind. In the pounding of waves on a beach, my parents heard the rush of the sea against the *Empire Brent's* prow. In the frilled ruffle of a Manly ferry's wake they saw the *Empire Brent's* wake as it dissolved and dispersed into the surrounding ocean.

The waves stretched into and broke upon our shores from the other side of the world, bringing with them a rush of memories. On the harbour, past the prosperous jacaranda-dusted gardens of Sydney's Eastern suburbs, across The Heads, past Dobroyd Point, my father flowed with stories of their passage along the Clyde and into the open sea. There was no turning back. They might never go home. Past the Rock of Gibraltar, the Mediterranean a glissando. Past Italy, Malta, Greece, though they stopped in none of those countries. Down the milky-blue corridor of the Suez Canal. We picnicked under Manly's Norfolk pines to tales of miners' union picnic days in Whitby or Scarborough or Blackpool. We built sandcastles. We swam, impressing parents who would never learn to swim. At dusk, we returned to a Circular Quay ringed by sandstone government buildings which glowed like the promised-land in the golden dusk. The Sydney Opera House was not yet built, but its foundations had replaced the old tram depot that once covered that site and its skeletal wings spoke of phoenixes.

The experience of migration divided the family generationally. My younger sister and I may have listened to the family stories eagerly, but we were Australian, while our older siblings were English. My English sister and brother seemed to bear the fingerprints of Yorkshire on them in ways my younger sister and I didn't. Couldn't. They were witnesses to this re-told family history in ways we Australian-born kids could never be. Their histories before Australia, before the new house, the garden, the Aussie schools and holidays, remained a fixed point of reference – somewhere we could visit whenever we needed clarification of an event or story that offered a different perspective on the family. Sunshine, abundant fresh food, beaches – these were ours as a birth right, while those older children were still chained to their memories, albeit fading, of life in a two-up, two-down in gloomy, wet, post-war Yorkshire.

We were in agreement though, in our understanding of our parents' journey. So brave. Such a great story. The family had travelled across a vast ocean and in doing so they had been inaugurated, transformed. They had carried the old world in them to the southern hemisphere. All that water they had crossed still pulsed in their veins. We were swept along with their sea narratives until we could fashion experiences of our own – on ferries, yachts, ocean liners, across the Pacific and the Indian oceans, when we inevitably went searching for our home.

CHAPTER TWO
Migrants from the North

'One does not discover new lands without consenting to lose sight, for a very long time, of the shore,' Andre Gide wrote in *The Counterfeiters*. My parents lost sight of their shore as the *Empire Brent* left Great Britain, then Europe, behind her, but a new shore soon sidled up to claim them. After leaving Fremantle, then Melbourne, the *Empire Brent* followed Australia's south eastern coastline, past Mallacoota in North Eastern Victoria to Eden, an old whaling station on the southernmost point of New South Wales. Past Bermagui and Merimbula, Pambula, Narooma and Bateman's Bay, past Wollongong and its northern beaches, Wombarra and Scarborough, where we would holiday as a family years later. Past Botany Bay, the first anchorage for Captain Phillips' convicts on the First Fleet. Through The Heads, past Nielsen Park and Rose Bay, under the Harbour Bridge to the industrial docks of Pyrmont. My family must have stood on the deck and watched as the bays and inlets, the little swipes of sandy beach, slowly passed. The children excited, the parents planning, wondering, getting anxious that soon they would disembark into the unknown.

I imagine my parents were full of apprehension as they prepared to leave the *Empire Brent* and enter their new life in Australia. Historians Kate Darian-Smith and Paula Hamilton see arrival as 'often a confusing and stressful time, so memories of the new country can be easily lost in the many years of settlement afterwards if they are not emphasised by those who help to shape the memories of migrants; and this begs the question, when do people stop being migrants?'

I see my family nervously gathering their cabin luggage and the souvenirs they'd bought in Suez – the pith helmet my father wore to protect himself from sunburn when gardening, the tooled leather handbag with camels and palm trees and pyramids worked into its flap, a little ashtray with *Empire Brent* printed on it. We touched these things reverentially all through my childhood, these relics of their journey. We created stories from them and used them for dressing up games.

Next, down the *Empire Brent's* gangplank, perhaps taking one last look at her as their eyes searched the crowd on the wharf for someone familiar. They may even have looked again at a photo of Uncle Mick, leaning against a car bonnet in some earlier black and white image. Their papers were stamped. They passed through the customs checks. They were reassured their trunks would be sent on later, and there he was, Mick, the unknown, the familiar, the man who would deliver them to their new life in his rickety old blue van.

From the wharves of Pyrmont, through the inner city, to the suburban streets of Western Sydney. On they drove. Past the shabby Victorian terrace houses of Erskineville, Newtown and St Peters which must have echoed with memories of similar houses in Wakefield and Barnsley. Did they reflect on the Australian government recruitment posters at this point – those primary-coloured images of sandy beaches and big brick bungalows, a Holden sedan in every driveway? Along Canterbury Road, past the mission-style Council Chambers, to Lakemba, Punchbowl, Bankstown. What were my parents thinking as they saw their new home – the sun, shining in a deep blue sky, illuminating, awarding everything a sharp focus?

I suspect they were wondering what the hell they'd done.

Uncle Mick was a man prone to moods, so his behaviour towards my family may have been welcoming and jocular, or it could just as easily have been taciturn. Either way, I suspect any conversation was subsumed into a reverie that comprised a soundtrack of my uncle's Australian accent, car horns, the whining of the van's engine, then a series of flashing images as the harbour receded, the streets became mean and narrow then widened again on the highway. The old Victorian-era houses were soon overtaken by new post-war housing – large plots, big grey-green gum trees, their branches enlivened by a gust of wind or the occasional white flash of a sulphur-crested cockatoo. The corner shops with their awnings and ice-cream signs, a child on a bike, a barking dog – all of these images spaced wide apart.

There is a point in migration when the migrant seems unsure of the path to take. They begin to question whether they have done the right thing. The way back is closed and the way forward is fraught with danger. They can no longer look ahead as they did on the sea voyage, when the vastness of the ocean extrapolated and expanded into optimism about their new life. Disembarkation brings with it a land-based reality. It is at this junction that migrants face their greatest existential crisis; alone, unsure, belonging nowhere. They grasp at epithets, carve a mythology of survival, of courage and struggle. These qualities might serve them well as they built their new lives in Australia, with its history of dogged persistence and battler bravery such as that forged in Gallipoli and the Somme in World War One. But Australian history could hardly offer comfort to the homesick and lonely immigrants who had just arrived from Europe and the UK. This crisis is not just a matter of being either of the old country or the new, but of dealing with the 'conflicting loyalties, family relationships and unresolved separation' that are common to the migrant experience, write Hammerton and Thomson.

I have always imagined that drive in my uncle's van was an anxious, regretful one – fearful emotions that stayed with my family for years. Over the coming months, as well as the loss of Yorkshire and their families in Royston, my parents needed to quickly come to terms with Australian culture, my father's new job, the bureaucracy of building a new house; struggling, as Gazmed Kapllani has written, to learn 'the rules of the game.' Kapllani believes:

(t)here is something heroic in the way a migrant abandons his native land. Nevertheless in his everyday life, he is fragile, confused, and at times ridiculous, like a card player who dreams of that one amazing trick but lacks essential knowledge of the rules of the game.

I used to believe that it was my mother, in a new country with two English children, who was most deeply perturbed by just which world she straddled. Where did she now belong? Was it her home in Yorkshire with its extended family, or this new one with our sponsoring relatives, my father's cousins, Margaret and Grace, their husbands, Mick and Peter, and their numerous children?

It wasn't our mother who was suffering the greatest despair, I know now. It was our father, who, despite his anxieties, or perhaps because of them, always seemed so hell bent on optimism – never look back, 'always look on the bright side', 'you'll never walk alone' – singing his way towards a utopian future with feel-better songs. Despite this jollity, he reached the crossroads of despair far earlier than my mother. According to my brother, it was Dad who sat on the bed, his head in his hands, weeping. 'What have I done?'

It was Dad who dragged himself out of bed every morning, dressing in the crowded space of the bedroom the family shared in my aunt's house. He collected his 'snap', the work lunch Mum had prepared and left on the kitchen table the night before, and headed off to work with Uncle Mick, no doubt wondering about Monkton pit and how his old workmates there were getting on. How did he manage this regret? I have a child's memory of him standing at a window and humming the anxiety away. Years later, whenever deeply troubled, he would stand at the bedroom window of his new house and, hands behind his back, stare out at the street through the slats of the Venetian blinds, still humming.

What else could someone do in an age before mass digital communication? My parents didn't have a telephone and anyway, a call to the UK would have been prohibitively expensive. Their £10 passage meant they had to stay for a statutory two years. This 'probation' period required assisted migrants who returned within two years to repay the balance of their outward fares in addition to their return fares. If my parents had succumbed to homesickness and gone back, they would have had to repay at least £120, a vast sum in those days. While a quarter of all British migrants did go back, my parents were made of stronger stuff than their homesickness might have indicated. They were bound to their new life, like it or not. Soldier on, make the most of it, my father's happy-go-lucky songs extolled, so they did.

All long sea voyages need larger-than-life heroes. My parents kept in touch with the friends they had made on the *Empire Brent* and all of them seemed to exemplify the heroic qualities associated with stepping off to a new place. The Tweedales came from Rochdale in Lancashire and the Shaws from Newcastle in Tyneside. Both couples also were travelling with small children. Once they had settled in Sydney, the families helped each other to build their houses and get jobs, all the while sharing harrowing or happy stories about their new country. They remained friends until they died, Charlie Shaw first, then Frank Tweedale – my parents outlived them by decades. As children, we went to Christmases and holiday lunches at their houses, the adults remembering the not-so-old days, invariably embellishing their stories about England or the voyage out while we children ate lunch on the back veranda and drank orange cordial from glasses adorned with stencils of Mickey Mouse. This was how I first discovered England, through myth-memories delivered by adults with strong Northern accents that still carried in them the whiff of pits and factories and all the verbal eccentricities of their origins. 'Sling thee hook', 'Owt to sup', 'Tek thee snap', 'Our lad, our lass', 'Pet', 'You don't get owt for nowt.' This talk fertilised our ideas about our lost nation. We were *new* Australians, even if that appellation was only supposed to refer to European migrants – the Italians and 'Balts' and Germans and Scandinavians and Dutch who had fled, just as the British had, to a better life in a new place.

Australia has a long history of failing to recognise the qualifications of its migrants; all those doctors, lawyers, accountants, academics, valued in their own countries, driving taxis in the new. Professionals patiently learned what they had to do to re-qualify, and spent years retraining – or gave up and accepted the government's imposed limitations, investing instead in their own children's education and building the opportunities for them they couldn't have for themselves.

My parents' friends talked of their new jobs in Australia, the way they had adapted skills honed in the coalfields of

County Durham or Yorkshire for factory jobs in Sydney. Like most migrants, they brought something of those old jobs with them – as 'Pommy' shop stewards in their trade unions, as experts in a range of machinery needed for new Australian industries, or a bluster and camaraderie that helped them negotiate relationships in a far more multicultural workforce than the ones they'd left behind in England. Their diverse skills helped build the economy of post-war Australia, and people like my parents and their friends were proud of the role they played. As Hammerton and Thomson explain about British migrants:

Most migrants had left school with only the basic qualifications, though many had acquired further training through apprenticeship in a trade. For example, between 1963 and 1973, 46% of the men were 'craftsmen and production process workers', and 41% of British women workers had clerical skills. In short, the migrants came from Britain's aspiring working and lower middle classes, and British immigration did indeed provide the skilled and semi-skilled workforce that Australia needed for post-war reconstruction.

The stories we overheard as children seemed tinged with sadness too. Watching the way my parents and their friends exchanged their memories, I couldn't help but reflect on how they wore their travel experiences like scars. This sense of bewilderment or divided loyalties seemed common amongst migrants: 'The war ended, we are free' wrote Polish migrant, Maria Lewitt in her novel, *No Snow in December*.

We have settled in Australia, where the standard of living is unparalleled by any country in the world. What puzzles me is this: why am I not completely happy? Why do I moan about the weather? Why can't I get used to gum trees instead of dreaming of pine forests and the crisp whiteness of December, January, February? Is it nostalgia?

History filled the air around my parents and their friends and their narratives became maps of Yorkshire, Durham and Lancashire, mines and mills and steelworks. Their mythologies also drifted with the sea, waves, storms and islands, and with character sketches of the other people on the *Empire Brent* who had been as brave as they had been to leave Barnsley, Tyneside, Manchester, Newcastle or Glasgow to cross vast oceans into the unknown. One narrative came through particularly loudly – the North. Their accents. Their clothes. Their humour. Their food. As well as their experiences on the *Empire Brent* – the shared Northerness of my parents and their friends offered a special kind of brother and sisterhood.

To this day, I feel that regional camaraderie, especially when I visit sites that celebrate northern achievement and identity such as Antony Gormley's powerful sculpture 'The Angel of the North' in Gateshead, just off the A1, the longest numbered road in the United Kingdom. The angel's towering height of 65 feet and its massive wings celebrate not only northern industry but also the wing-spread of northerners across the UK and the world. Gormley has said his sculpture is representative of the region's hopes and fears. Others, such as the art critic, Paul Nicholson, define it differently:

The Angel's broad open wings appear to welcome you to the region – or home. In contrast when looking at its back from the north, it appears to take on the guise of a guardian Angel whose outstretched wings protect those inside its territory from hostile forces.

The North. We are from THE NORTH. This remained the family mantra. From our earliest years my younger sister and I, both of us born in Sydney, learned we were Northerners and we should be proud of it. I don't think this was ever said quite as emphatically as I have written it. If it was, I can't recall the exact words spoken or how they were delivered. What was clear though was our heritage; that constant immersion in Northerness, the references to Yorkshire, the accents, the memories, the food and customs. Where exactly is the North? I must have asked that question dozens of times. This was pointless, I realised as an adult: the North was a geographical region in England that resided in Bankstown, and in my parents, as powerfully as it had when they lived in Royston.

In his book *Pies and Prejudice: In Search of the North*, Stuart Maconie jokes: 'According to legend, the North begins at the RAC Traffic Centre on the M6 just at the point where the road surface changes from tarmac to cobbles.' Maconie also cites the journalist and satirist, Michael Winner, who believed that the north began at London's Oxford Circus. Maconie takes some comfort from the Lonely Planet Guide's claim that the north begins in Derbyshire near Bakewell, where 'the soft chalkiness of southern England starts to stiffen with grit and limestone; there are proper ridges, escarpments and big bleak brawny moors.'

These matters of geography were never explored by my parents. No definition was needed. They had all the credentials: cloth caps, pits, parkin, Yorkshire puddings, accents. As a small child, these must have been accepted as the norm and I certainly don't recall finding anything in my parents' behaviour odd at that stage. My family just did what James Woods describes as gorging on nostalgia, 'with a fondness that might have embarrassed' us had we actually lived in the North of England.

My embarrassment came later when I began making comparisons with my school friends' parents, especially those who were born or raised in Australia and therefore could claim an Australian pedigree of a generation or two. What they ate and how they lived didn't bear comparison. We were the only family from Yorkshire that I knew of, though my friends included the children of Scots and Irish as well as European families. We constantly asked our parents to tell us about the sweets they ate as children, taking a kind of drooling delight in the pear drops, raspberry chews and sherbet fountains. We ate black pudding and offal, chips with every meal, Pomfret cakes and parkin and that made us rather unique.

The food of migrants, writes Aleksandar Hemon, stands for:

> the authentic life we used to live, which is no longer available except as a model for this new, elsewhere life. It is therefore important that the food-related practices from the previous life be reconstructed in the new context. The food, if made properly, might be where authenticity is partially restored, despite the displacement.

Migrants may make the foods of home but it 'inescapably ends up having the taste of displacement.' What other child's mother cooked Yorkshire parkin to consume at cracker night bonfires, or offered stories about pits and ponies in a flat, droning South Riding accent? I may not have known exactly where the North was located but it was served up on every plate. It hung over every conversation or memory. I knew it resided inside my family and in everything we did, be it a picnic or cinema visit or a day at the beach. Somehow, in each of our social interactions, Yorkshire couldn't help but make its presence felt.

Most of these encounters involved a Yorkshire tradition – my father's stories about childhood games or my mother queuing for bread and jam with the other miners' children at food banks set up to assuage hunger during the Great Strike of 1926. We knew the names of famous Yorkshire cricketers and footballers and the proud history of Barnsley Football Club which had won the FA Cup in 1912. Every Sunday evening we ate dinner to a radio program, *The Christie's Music Hour*. Christie's was an umbrella shop in Sydney's Pitt Street, a Scottish company, and the hour featured popular music from Scotland. I have memories of salads and despicable herrings in tomato sauce, a meal deemed 'light' because we'd eaten a far heavier Sunday lunch after Sunday school, which always comprised a roast joint – lamb or beef – with roast vegetables and Yorkshire pudding and a thick gravy fashioned from the meat juices. A light Sunday evening meal was all that was needed to accompany the songs of Andy Stewart or Kenneth McKeller. Before the Christie's hour we needed to sit silently, no knives scraping plates, no whining about the herrings, because the BBC World Service football results were being broadcast. So we watched as our father listened intently, noting the results in the kind of little black incident notebook I would afterwards always associate with Brian Blessed playing a cop on TV's *Z Cars*.

Liverpool 1 – Manchester United 0
Crystal Palace 2 – Sheffield Wednesday 1
Leeds United 1 – Tottenham Hotspur 0

On and on the scores went through the various divisions, including the Scottish league, while our buttered bread dried and curled. Where are these places, I wondered; Tottenham Hotspur, Crystal Palace, Arsenal, Sheffield Wednesday, Everton, Heart of Midlothian? It was Leeds United that mattered though, and I was glad in the 1970s to be able to bear back to Australia – with all the pride of a captured Roman Eagle – some Leeds United club paraphernalia for my father.

The north. Hammerton and Thomson argue that 'assimilationist ideology generally assumes a fading commitment of later generations to the migrant identity.' This fails to take account of the ways in which identity is shaped by sentimentality, history, empathy with parents and siblings, a desire to be truly 'of' a mixed family in which some are from the old country and others from the new one. Commitment is forged in identities like this – that mix of what is shared and what was missed out on, the romantic imagining of the place that wasn't quite yours.

This dichotomy was abetted by the numerous links and resources that fed our commitment to England. We devoured articles in *The Dalesman*, that magazine of Yorkshire life established in 1939 and still in publication to this day. Over the years, writers such as J.B. Priestley, Alan Bennett and Ian McMillan contributed to it. It arrived in the mail, bringing with it in all its articles a little Yorkshire symphony of lost sounds and smells and voices and landscape. As we scrutinised its illustrated pages, the north became a place so imbued with memory it felt like a knitted sock, circular and holy, fashioned out of thick, utilitarian wool.

'Young Fred', a column written by Will Clemence in the vernacular of the Dales, added to our sense of belonging in that northern space. The column's laconic humour didn't seem particularly funny to me as a child, but my parents found it hilarious. It was exotic but understood because it came from that part of Yorkshire through which they'd cycled or rambled, returning afterwards to their cramped mining village. Whenever I visit Yorkshire these days, I wonder how those two different Yorkshires blended and re-formed themselves in my parents' memories – theirs of the pit towns and the other of the men and women with their sheep farms in the Dales. How different they were, but something must have connected them – Northernness certainly, but also a love of their county, however privileged or poor they were in their access to it.

My family made its transition from sea traveller to new migrant slowly, just as the *Empire Brent's* constant noise, the perpetual pulse of her engines, slowly faded. They lived with Aunt Margaret and Uncle Mick in their 1920s weatherboard house in Bankstown for two years, until they built a temporary house – a garage, then the fibro house that would remain their home until my mother left it sixty years later for a nursing home when she was in her nineties. Bankstown was a mix of houses, people, bushland and industry. It had been named after Captain Cook's botanist, Joseph Banks, and it still bore the relics of its former indigenous Bidjigal community in place names like 'Black Charlie's Hill', and of earlier settlers whose old Victorian and Edwardian houses were flanked by new fibrous cement ones such as my parents were intending to build.

My Aunt Margaret and Uncle Mick and their six daughters – the last and seventh would arrive a few years after me – lived a few doors away, up a little hill that was topped by a small, general-purpose store from which my mother ordered most of our food. Meat was bought from a butcher a few blocks away. A bus into Bankstown's shops stopped at a nearby corner, which was handy for parents who didn't have a car. Relatives and neighbours kindly drove us to places we could not visit on public transport for picnics and outings, or to their own houses for lunch.

Frank Tweedale was always kind in that regard. He would arrive at my parents' house in his old Morris Minor and in we would pile for the trip to his home in Merrylands. This was one of the places where I eavesdropped on all the adults' northern stories while drinking sticky sweet cordial from a Mickey Mouse glass. Being a migrant seemed a natural state of affairs. There were too many migrants in Bankstown for it not to be. We migrants were all in the same boat – or so it felt to me as a child – whether English or of other nationalities. To this day, Bankstown remains one of the most ethnically diverse municipalities in Australia, with more recent migrants from Vietnam, Lebanon, Somalia, China and Pakistan adding to the mix of countries from the post-war period.

Bankstown may have seemed a long way removed from the *Empire Brent*'s sea voyage to Australia, but England had travelled with my parents too, and they carried homesickness within them, nestling low under their ribs like a misplaced heart. My father had a fine tenor voice so as well as singing his keep-up-your-spirits songs, he keened his homesickness away in the ballads he'd sing from the bathroom, 'I'll Take You Home Again Kathleen', or sentimental love songs from musicals or light opera like Franz Lehar's 'You are My Heart's Delight'. His melancholy renderings of these songs seeped like steam from the bathroom where he sang as he shaved before the mirror. To this day I cannot hear them without feeling the pall of his homesickness descend. For migrants like my father, homesickness planted itself in 'the unbridgeable fissure opened between the self and the environment... When a person finds themselves unable to act: one takes refuge in the memories of the past from the potentially traumatizing encounter with the present' as Ghassan Haghe has written.

This homesickness and nostalgia opened up like an old wound whenever a new parcel arrived from the UK, initiating me into the nostalgia too; though unlike my migrant older brother and sister, I had no prior claim on England. Inside the parcels were comics, *Topper, Beano* and *Dandy*, which, once read by our Yorkshire cousins, were neatly rolled up and secured with a rubber band and posted out to us. There were hair grips and hand knits for my sister and me. Books, English sweets, including Kendal Mint cake, bullseyes and those Pomfret cakes so beloved of Dad. *The Barnsley Chronicle* and *The Dalesman* were included too, which my father read avidly from cover to cover, though he'd never been one of those cloth-capped, pipe-smoking, laconic sheep farmers we saw in the magazine's photos, those Dales men leaning over farm gates. Each parcel that arrived from my grandmother or aunts reinforced our Yorkshire identity by beguiling and teasing us with these iconic Yorkshire offerings. The parcels' contents transported us from suburban Sydney with its gum trees and kookaburras, its heat and cicadas: one moment we were in hot, dry western Sydney then suddenly we were in a coal-scented back-to-back, or a rolling Dales' landscape punctuated by dry stone walls dusted with snow.

Does migration require mediation in situations like this? Are former lives more assertively calibrated to ensure that newer family members, unburdened by a past history, don't get too far ahead of everyone else in the new country? I would suggest that the family history needs to be paced, modulated and refined, reiterated, agreed upon and that the past needs to be embroidered into the family's spare, new tapestry. Stories are told and retold until the details are agreed upon. This historical grounding always reminded me of films of prisoners in some German Stalag. This is what you must remember – this is what you get right. Written on rice paper. Remembered. Consumed. If they torture you, at least you all have the same narrative. The French philosopher, Marc Auge likened this memorializing to a gardener's task of selecting and pruning. 'Memories are like plants: there are those that need to be quickly eliminated in order to transform: between the seeds and the cuttings from which they were born and what they have become there is hardly any apparent relationship anymore.'

Blanco, Caicedo and Loranzo write in their tribute to the Special Broadcasting Service's broadcaster, Alberto Dominguez, that this historical reframing is an essential part of how migrants determine who they are:

For most of us, every stage of our lives weaves a new layer of self into our personal history, redefining the answers to the essential questions of who we are, where we've come from and where we're headed. For migrants, the struggle for identity and belonging is threefold. Our sense of self is fragmented: we are who we were back home, who we are now, as perceived in the wider collective of our newly adopted country, and we are also who we epitomise in our community.

The chorus to this process for my family was formed from the people who called to us from over the sea like sea nymphs in some Jasonian myth. We had numerous photos of family. All the old, dead relatives with their quirks and secrets. My parents had living brothers and sisters and cousins left behind but doing quite nicely, thank you, now Mr Attlee and the Labour Party were in charge. Letters prolonged this two-way mediation – this 'I'll send you mine, if you send me yours' boasting. 'To take a photo is to have an interest in things as they are' wrote Susan Sontag in *On Photography* and so photography became our family's new narrative, immediate, proud, regretful. Wedding photos. An aunt's snaps of holidays in Blackpool or Scarborough or Bridlington were compared with my family's holidays in shacks beside Tuggerah Lakes or by the sea at Toowoon Bay.

George Kovaros sees these photographic exchanges as ways of refashioning experience so it appears 'commonplace or part of the natural order of things,' the photographs helping to facilitate a connection between two histories, two worlds, complicit yet also distinct. I would also argue that the photographs take a more visceral role; they are the anxious hugs or physical contact unavailable to us, a kind of photographic touchstone through which a migrant allays their fears of loss. 'Migrants live with the acute, heart-breaking certainty that every family visit may be the final embrace,' write Blanco, Caicedo and Loranzo. Photographs offer this embrace on paper: a poor substitute, admittedly, but one that brings, at least, distant loved ones into a new home.

So back and forth our photographic comparisons flew between Whitby and Pontefract and Fountains Abbey and Taronga Park Zoo, Manly Beach, Paddy's Market or Centennial Park by tram. We scrutinised what our English cousins were doing with the same curiosity with which they were no doubt scrutinising our photos – longing for beaches and sunshine as enviously as we longed for outings to Barnsley and coal fires and school meals and snowy Christmases.

Slowly, these stories of our relatives in England trickled through. Some of my parents' siblings moved away from Yorkshire – down south mostly, that trek taken by so many northerners from the impoverished north to southern cities and towns where jobs were more plentiful. My mother's siblings, in particular, seemed to be drawn to places by the sea. One brother moved to Margate and two sisters headed for Bournemouth and Christchurch. When I first visited them, I was surprised by these choices. Those shabby sea-side towns of the 1970s seemed to be no better than the places in Yorkshire the family had left. But as well as white collar jobs, the towns had the sea and sand, alongside once-grand ballrooms and bingo parlours; perhaps these made my uncles and aunts feel more festive and holiday-spirited. While visiting, I would often go for solitary walks along the beach; the wind blustery, the waves tenuous. It always seemed cold, so where better to retreat than to a tearoom on the end of a long Edwardian pier, to gaze through steam-frosted windows at the grey sky outside while drinking a cup of perniciously strong tea.

My uncle and I once walked from Margate to Broad-stairs on a summer's Sunday that challenged my prejudices against English beaches. The sun was hot, the sky a Wedgwood blue. We gazed across the English Channel to France, before following in Dickens' footsteps past the ghosts of characters from *David Copperfield* and *Bleak House*. Later, we sat in a pub that was all plush red velvet walls and leather chesterfields. By the time we were ready to walk home, the afternoon sun had picked up the distant chalk cliffs of the French coast. A hovercraft was gliding across the water towards Calais or Boulogne.

We took some fish and chips back with us – it was still a small wonder for me to know that, unlike in Australia,

English 'chippies' only fried at certain times of the day and an order was worded 'cod and chips twice.' I always enjoyed saying it. What a miracle Broadstairs seemed, this small golden Dickensian place. Fish and chips freshly battered and fried. Beaches and gulls and literary references and characterful pubs, so doggedly English despite Broadstairs' tantalising proximity to France.

I described it all to my parents in gushing terms on the back of a postcard. The little sandy cove of Broadstairs beach, a couple of donkeys saddled up and ready for riders. There was something showy in my postcards and letters home now. An explorer's diary, a ship's log. Neither parent had ever been to this part of England, so I had the added responsibility of capturing it for them. Not as it really was, but how they imagined it to be. I wrote of those sunny days as though from Paradise. I sent a photo of my uncle and aunt leaning against the hull of some wealthy person's speedboat, their grey hair swept back by a blustery wind. My mother's family were living the kind of life she could have lived if she just had not gone so far away. 'See,' each postcard seemed to say. Just a few hundred miles down to Hampshire or Kent was all it took, not 12,000 miles to Sydney.

These were visits where I also gleaned stories of my parents when they were children or teenagers. Being one of the oldest meant my Margate uncle was a font of information about my mother. I listened as though my life depended on it – so many questions answered, so many conundrums solved. That shy girl in family pictures, or the photo with seven of the ten children, when my mother stands in a defiant pose – the only one I ever saw her take. What was she thinking when the camera shutter clicked? What made her seem so different from the girl in other images? My uncle described her as shy and stubborn, secretive, frightened.

She didn't ever stand up to her parents as he had done, storming out of the house one day after a fight with his father, and never going back. These little patches of my mother began to take shape like a brightly-coloured and memory-laden quilt. She was all those things as an adult: she hadn't changed a lot. The girl had become a woman frozen in the amber of the life she'd left behind.

I found myself walking the beaches with her. Through pleasure gardens planted with pink begonias. Through the penny arcades with their penny shove machines. Past the rock shops. Her brother said she lived for outings that took her away from the family home in Royston and the middle child responsibility of caring for younger siblings. She must have run along wet sand or built sandcastles on those miners' picnic days in Scarborough or Bridlington. Let the wind tease her hair out of its hairgrips. Spun and laughed and expanded into the ozone freedom of it. So I wrote long letters to the child as well as the mother, knowing she wanted to hear of the childish things she had put aside but needed to live again from an alien place. This suspicion was confirmed when she visited England with my father, and again after he died. She headed to places like Bournemouth and Scarborough and Blackpool and had a whale of a time. She indulged herself with ice-creams and fairground rides, won useless prizes at Bingo. In the photos of these trips, you can see the girl under the aged face and white hair, making up for lost time.

One of my uncles on my father's side moved to the Isle of Man, and his children and grandchildren live there to this day. It was to visit them that I first passed through Liverpool, little knowing, as I boarded the boat to Douglas at Liverpool's Pier Head, that I would live and work in

Liverpool one day. My father's other brother, Fred, stayed on in Yorkshire and he is buried in the little cemetery in Havercroft. His children travelled to other countries too and I remember when first meeting him, silenced momentarily by his uncanny resemblance to my father, how he spoke wistfully of the geographical distance between him and his son in Africa as he made a ham salad for our tea.

All that travel, all the separating of families into geographical components. We became a map, a jigsaw puzzle to be shuffled, scrutinised and put together again, but not until each piece had been considered individually and as a whole. The world made tiny, then large again. So many places, so many miles. Yet here was my uncle buried only minutes from where he had been born, had lived his whole life; a small unassuming grave for a life that had seen so many changes, so many departures, yet remained tethered to place.

And what did I know of my grandparents? Very little. My father's mother was designated feisty but I'm not sure by whom. She was a worrier and deeply superstitious. Her older sons were teasers and they loved to play tricks on her. Once, knowing her to be sewing by the fire in the kitchen, they hung a jar from the window above and lowered it with a lighted candle in it. They bumped it against the glass of the kitchen window, frightening her half to death as the light swung backwards and forwards in a ghostly arc. Another time one of Dad's brothers heated a penny edge and ran the coin across his sleeping older brother's throat. The boy woke believing his throat had been cut and bellowed the house down. These jokes contain a sadism I find troubling, but in the days before television or social media, I suppose they just passed as boisterous fun.

More troubling was one of my mother's uncles who kept rabbits. He asked my cousin, then three or four years old,

which rabbit was his favourite. When my cousin selected, he took the animal from its cage and broke the rabbit's neck in front of the startled child. They ate the rabbit
for dinner that night. Backwards and forwards these stories passed. They frightened me when I first heard them.
They were gothic, I recognise now, akin to the behaviour
of Heathcliffe in *Wuthering Heights*. No wonder so many
family members couldn't wait to escape Yorkshire's grip.
The stories also spoke of the cusp age, between the wars,
when living conditions in Yorkshire's mining villages were
still Victorian and dehumanising. People died underground
or toiled in appalling conditions. They were hungry and
angry and these emotional states coloured a gloomy view of
life. That is what we Australian children used to joke about
our parents until we reached a more sympathetic adulthood
– 'Excuse the glum humour,' we would laugh. 'It's just that
they're from Yorkshire.'

My father's father is a mystery. I know he was called Walter and that is about all I know. I was never curious about
him, and my father never revealed anything that might il-
luminate his father's life. I felt curious though, as I wandered through the Barnsley Heritage Museum, wishing
I'd pushed my father to tell me more. Four generations of
my father's family are called Walter. My great-grandfather,
grandfather, uncle and cousin. There is something Monty
Pythonesque about the repetition of it. It's a working-class
version of the regnal naming system, played for laughs, or
perhaps just for generational dignity. A photo of all four
generations of Walters was taken in the garden in Royston.
Great-grandfather Walter is wearing a homburg hat and
Grandfather Walter a flat cap. Young Walter is hatless and
baby Walter in his arms is hatless too, his baby hair standing on end in the breeze.

'All happy families resemble one another,' Leo Tolstoy wrote in *Anna Karenina*, 'and each unhappy family is unhappy in its own way.' Our passed-on family stories had quickly taken on the distortions and embellishments of Chinese whispers. What to believe, what to see as fiction? My mother's family seemed tinged with unhappiness. Her father could have been the child of one of those Victorian novels run though with cruelty. His father had remarried after his mother died and, like all the evil stepmothers of fairy tales, this new mother abused him. So did his father. When my mother mentioned once that her father didn't like to be seen without his shirt I asked why. 'Because he had stripes,' she replied. I could only think of the words from the Bible or the chorus in Handel's *Messiah*. 'Stripes?' I asked. 'Yes, you know. Scars.' 'But how did he get them?' And so the story began.

In his article 'The Meaning and Meaninglessness of Genealogy,' Nathan Lents argues against any obsession with family history, especially genetics. 'In order to celebrate our past,' he writes, 'is it really necessary to know who is descended from whom?'

The history of our culture is written in the some-times-mundane, sometimes-heroic stories of our families. The stories are important and they belong to us all.

As I listened to my family stories on that first trip to England, I felt I was being inducted into a special order. I sat, absorbing characters as though they were parts of me, ghosts made flesh. My grandfather's story seemed to answer a lot of questions about where my mother's side of the family had come from and how his cruel history had been passed on.

At the time of his abuse, my great-grandfather was running a hotel. My grandfather, then aged about ten, was in charge of the horses. He tied them to the railings in the hotel's yard and kept an eye out to ensure all was well. Something happened; I'm not sure what, but a horse got away or became distressed or may have been injured. As a punishment, my grandfather was tied to the horse rail and whipped until his back was shredded and bleeding. He carried the scars all his life, on his back and mentally. He left his cruel home as soon as he could.

From what my mother told me, he was a man of sadism too. He fought with his children, keeping a cane at the dining table to lash out with if anyone misbehaved. He paid no heed to my mother's tears. She hated being late for school, but he would send her on pre-school errands anyway, guaranteeing punishment when she finally arrived at her class. He was never affectionate, never proud of his kids. The older boys left home. My mother and her sister went to live in at the hospital in Ilkley where they worked as nurses. Like most bullies, he was frightened. He hid under the stairs during thunderstorms; was uncertain and anxious, marinating a fatalism that found voice in his numerous truisms. When his daughters told him they were getting married he shrugged and said, 'you make your bed and lie in it.' I expect my mother received the same response when she told him that she and her husband and children were migrating to Australia. All his children knew that whatever life threw at them they could never go home.

When I heard these stories, I scrutinised anew the few photos we had of him. He just looked like a benign, white-haired old man, and I have often wondered if the stories didn't do him justice. Perhaps he wasn't a nasty, damaged man at all, just a badly mythologised one. The vast distance between the man and his offspring must have taken some kind of toll. He lost his youngest son while still a child, and his oldest daughter to tuberculosis. She left behind a husband and her kids. Did my grandfather grieve them? Did he stand at the gate and wait for letters from my mother in Australia or the daughters in Kent and Hampshire? Did he ever wish he had been kinder? Any letters he wrote to my mother are long gone, so he remains a mystery, a photograph; the man whose death made my mother weep in the kitchen of our new house in Bankstown, while I drew pictures at the kitchen table.

As for the other relatives – those shadow people on the edges of family photos – they remain a mystery too, even more so now there is no one to ask for information about them. The fading photos of men in hats, the child with the violin, the wedding guests, the old man with a baby. The handsome man in an RAF uniform. The nurse, the girl in a fancy-dress costume, the little boy on a rocking horse. History has anonymised them and so, as I have since I was a child poring over the old photo box, I feel free to make up whatever I like about them.

In his autobiography Roland Barthes states, 'everything herein must be considered as though spoken by a character in a novel.' When I was a child, there were times when our Yorkshire history became a burden and I felt I was a character in a novel about a migrant family. It just felt oppressive to be an Australian player in such a British narrative. The cultural differences were what most strikingly held us down, that sense that everything we did had to travel to our contemporary lives in Bankstown via Royston and that it was consumed, digested, regurgitated along the way so that the received story, when it finally arrived, bore little resemblance to anything we could understand. My Lithuanian and Italian and Spanish friends had similar experiences, and although we didn't speak about them in depth or specificity, they surfaced in an odd sense of discord, like an out of tune piano. We were torn between emotions that felt uncanny, unsettled, especially as we reached the hypersensitivity of adolescence and the desperate need to conform. Pity, envy, embarrassment, shame, frustration; these were the common emotions we so often directed at our parents.

As with so many migrant families, this was, as George Kouvaros has written, a time of 'strange behaviours, a time when we were all exposed to the cost of our emotions'. These feelings were refined in adulthood, as a clearer understanding of our backgrounds made sense of the past – especially in the light of Australian Prime Minister Gough Whitlam's multicultural policies – but for a long time they seemed insurmountable and caused a growing generational rift. Why couldn't our parents just be *normal* and fit in, like everybody else?

I write backwards from an adulthood that has provided numerous opportunities for travel in Europe, Southeast Asia and the UK. I try to capture my child-self before this geographical expansion, at school, with my child's 'local' worldview. Intrinsic to this is an understanding of the ways in which my parents travelled through their adopted southern landscape of suburban Sydney. The newly built post-war housing that mushroomed between older houses. Those mysterious Victorian or Edwardian houses that offered echoes of history and permanence in the new place. Someone, at some time, built those houses while my parents and their ancestors were living in Yorkshire. With curiosity, we passed stained glass windows and Victorian verandas. So – people were here before us, before post-war migration, before making do in garages while building new fibro houses. 'What is it like to be born in a place, to stay and live there, to know you are of it…' asked Edward Said, and viewing Bankstown's pre-war houses, we asked that question too.

Migration offers only a snail house. You carry your old house with you. Homes left behind. New homes furnished with items carried over the seas, new pieces or second-hand ones bearing the patina of someone else's life. I can recite the items we recycled from friends of the family: the Victorian kitchen table, the mismatched kitchen chairs, the wooden bed that my mother painted white and covered with transfers of ballerinas in blue tutus. The Bakelite radio. The concrete washing tubs. Our toys and clothes were stored in the trunks that had been carried onto the *Empire Brent*, stuffed with those books too treasured to be left behind: for my parents these included their Sunday school prizes and *The Golden Treasury*.

This cultural shaping has stayed with my family and a new generation has laid its own claim to it. We get teary when we hear a brass band from a once-proud mining village. We can mimic a joke Yorkshire accent. We still eat parkin, though we rarely make our own. We occasionally wear a flat cap; some of my father's very old ones are still in good condition, a comment on the quality of wool and manufacture lost when the caps went elsewhere for production. It is impossible to write this without sentimentality. Is a northern identity more prone to morose feelings of loss and struggle, a hardness of character with a soppy, sentimental core that melts and liquifies to specific northern prompts? The former *Guardian* journalist, Martin Wainwright, sees the north and northern identity as 'both our glory and our problem. It is the land,' he says:

that gave birth to all the clichés – dark, grim, cobbled and the rest of it – because in its heyday they were true. No part of England has had a stronger character, and you do not part with that sort of reputation easily. Huge mills, smoking chimneys, mass workforces; they were all there and sometimes you think, despairingly, that they will cling on indelibly forever.

This clinging to place – what Wainwright calls the 'excessive rootedness of Yorkshire' – comes, he admits, from the close bonds forged in single-industry communities, allowing them to pass into a northern lore that will not let them die. While this deep-rootedness of community and industries lost plays an important part in contemporary arguments about identity and place, the migration of Yorkshire to other parts of the world also keeps the county alive. A few generations ago, post-war Yorkshire travelled to the Southern Hemisphere, to Sydney, to Bankstown with my family and there it rests in our generational histories and the retelling of family stories.

A migrant's internalised country is also a static identity in so many ways, as migrants returning to Italy or Malta, Latvia or Germany or England will acknowledge. 'Return is never easy ... and places of the heart rarely stay the same,' Hammerton and Thomson assert. Places move on, modernise, are shaped by their own incoming migrants or economic or political shifts that render them unrecognisable when migrants return for a visit. For migrants going back to the old place, the past 'exists in the present, but elsewhere,' infiltrating their everyday lives as a form of 'spatial haunting' specific to the diasporic condition.

Ian Baucom argues that the 'nation for which one is nostalgic, rather than the nation one inhabits, is a closed narrative, an accomplished act.' Idealisation is also the glue to this process, a fixative which binds the past into one of those old daguerreotype photos you see of grand European cities before the war. Black and white, it is hard to imagine the colour and flux and vivacity of the real and pulsating city.

It is up to the hybrid generation, those first footers into a new place, to show how both old and new place can be claimed. Refusing to go home at all, James Wood asserts, is a way for the migrant to say, 'I couldn't go back home because I wouldn't know how to anymore.' Those who do return, he says, experience a kind of 'masquerade ... as if (I) were putting on my wedding suit, to see if it still fits.'

My family's northerness sat oddly in Bankstown, and I often wonder what our sponsoring Aunt Margaret and Uncle Mick made of it – or our neighbours, some of whom had once been migrants too. These included the Andersons next door on the right, who had come to Australia from Scotland after the First World War, and the Gracies who ran the little shop up the hill and had come from London's East End. Others had been Australian for enough generations to lay claim to an identity that would not be ours for a long time, like the Charltons on the left who hailed from the area around Orange on the western slopes of the Blue Mountains, and who clearly believed we children needed rescuing from our parents' old-world habits and accents. When my younger sister was born, Mrs Charlton took it upon herself to educate the toddler on the right way to speak, asking her to repeat the word 'bucket' over and over again until it was cleansed of its Yorkshire pronunciation – 'bookit'. Such was the hold of my parents' accents that they continued to shape our pronunciation a decade into our childhoods, and they never spoke with anything other than a profound Barnsley accent until the day they died.

To assuage his homesickness for Royston, my father was drawn to places that reminded him of Yorkshire. Paddy's Market in Sydney's Haymarket district became the Barnsley Market of his memory. Paddy's – with its stalls, garrulous old women stallholders, bread and scones, its second-hand clothes, extra-sharp knives, rabbits and chickens; their shit so acidic it caused my eyes to water. Each step was a step through my father's past, those chicken feathers floating between Northern and Southern hemispheres of memory. Their chickens, ours, my sister gagging because the smell of them made her nauseous. Not haggling, as his Aunt Kate had done in Barnsley Market – my father was far too shy for that – but Aunt Kate travelled with him nevertheless, her favourite sugar baby nephew, seeking, until he died, anything that reminded him of home.

On visits to Paddy's we got off the train at Central Station and walked the Devonshire Street tunnel to Railway Square. I'm sure this was for the novelty of the tunnel's tiled and resonant space. If we were lucky, we might return via Central station's departure hall for country trains with its glass roof, courting pigeons and giant clock. 'This is what the station in Leeds is like,' my father would say.

Sheffield.

Wakefield.

Huddersfield.

York.

There were no misty mornings when the rush of steam from a train met the chill of a Northern winter, no porters in flat caps, none of the Yorkshire bustle we'd heard about.

Sydney's Central station impressed us though, because it was so like my brother's English Hornby trains. It was just the destinations that were different. Deniliquin and Tamworth and Werris Creek and Narrabri and Dubbo spoke of the dust-dry country of the New South Wales western slopes or the New England district, with its wheat and sheep like those Macarthur merinos we drew in our geography books at school. Even the country people waiting with bags and parcels seemed to come from an Australia that would never really be ours. We ran into them at Sydney's Royal Easter Show where they proudly exhibited cattle and cakes and jam and strode around as though they owned the place – and back then, when Australia's wealth was riding on the sheep's back, I suppose they did.

Central. Which way to turn? The Devonshire Street tunnel or Eddy Avenue with its big old trees, then Campbell Street with its Chinese shops? If we chose Campbell Street, we enjoyed the added bonus of Chinatown. Heat palpitated off the footpath as we passed Mah-jong parlours or a Chinese child playing with a doll we regarded rudely and compared with our own. The market's proximity saw lacquered ducks on hooks and stacks of fruit in front of the shops. The exoticism of the Chinese traders made us feel more comfortable in our own difference.

My mother outlived my father by 22 years. When he turned 70, Dad joked that he had reached his biblical lot of three score years and ten. He made it to 76 but my mother went on to 95, by then a girlish version of her former self, remembering none of her children's names but finding us amusing just the same. Her Yorkshire accent remained undiminished. When we were kids, she was the kind of woman who was always making something; our clothes, stuffed toys, tablecloths and rugs, so she was a great boon to school fete committees. She made dolls' clothes and felt brooches and bookmarks – all sold for a few shillings to add to the school coffers in an era when working class schools relied on parents to help with the cost of maintaining the school grounds or funding the library or student outings. In an age before digital media and the ever-present expectation of work, twenty-four hours a day, parents like my mother had time to do their bit with their hands.

Whenever I visited my mother in her care home – her stories long disappeared into the fog of her dementia – I wished I could share a few more memories with her. Like my father, my mother had been a great storyteller and she filled our heads with tales from her own childhood in Royston. She also was a source of stories about the life lived by my older siblings before they migrated. Through her I was gifted the image of my brother's bare bottom on the chilly slate kitchen sink in Royston – the shock of icy slate on bare skin was a sure way to stop him holding his breath as he cried. Or the sugar pigs and wine gums on sale in the village shop. I hold her responsible for my romanticizing of England, especially the Victorian house on the green in which she grew up with her nine siblings and her cruel father. It all smacked of Ethel Turner's book, *Seven Little Australians*, but became so much more real than the Australian narrative because it contained a history that was generationally ours. None of this entered her childhood stories, though. The past, the left behind, had to be idealized.

I sometimes dream about those early years when I was born into a family still caught between two worlds, the old and the new. In my dreams, I am that new, Australian-born child standing at a door, looking out, looking in, and I feel an adult's weight of responsibility on my shoulders because I belong to both spaces and I have a specific and important role to play, rather like a translator or a tour guide. Perhaps this is why, like my father, I used to carry anxiety and an overburdening sense of my responsibilities with me whenever I went out with my parents. Everything must go right, because if it doesn't it will be my fault. As a toddler, I'm sure I negotiated between my siblings' ways of establishing themselves in a new country and my natural birth right to it. It was an odd feeling, heavily tinted with a kind of cultural embarrassment.

Despite this, before long we became Australian. Brown. Chirpy. Opinionated. Sporty. All remain qualities I associate with my place of birth. I joke about them here in Liverpool. 'Forgive me,' I say to colleagues. 'That was a very Australian thing to say.' People smile as they do when I joke about the cricket or the rugby – sports in which I share no interest at all unless Australia is winning against England. In this practice, I see I have been schooled well. I learned in those early years in Bankstown how to fashion an Australian self despite the heavy hand of Yorkshire. Day in, day out, from school to childish games, the sweet rituals and fallings-in-love of adolescence, the apologetic self-consciousness of a young adulthood when a parent had to be explained as though their Northernness held an answer to ancient runes. 'Forgive my mum and dad,' I'd say to friends, or 'beware – my father might bore you with stories about Barnsley football club.' My friends would nod politely, though they liked both parents very much. How foolish we are when we fail to see the qualities that others see easily. Migration adds an extra and redundant level of sensitivity.

Growing up in such a divided way, loyalty torn between this country and that, was character-forming in its own way. It certainly offered a duality that I still find useful; I have convinced myself, at least, that I can see both sides of my cultural heritage. I believe I am pragmatically able to speak from both. And I have never lost my pride in the

North, especially in Liverpool where it offers an extra level of credentialing – if being Australian cuts no extra weight, then my Yorkshire heritage might just do it.

CHAPTER THREE
Home

To leave *home*, to go to a new *home*, to build your own *home*: the word 'home' took on new meaning as my family resettled in Australia. As soon as they'd arrived their thoughts turned to building a house. They weren't alone in this impulse. Hammerton and Thomson believe acquiring your first home by purchase, or building your own, is 'often the most vividly-remembered story of the early years in Australia':

Fondly recalled struggles to attain the first home form something of a recurring motif in the migrant life story, reminiscent of pioneer narratives, eclipsing negative experiences and regrets. The vividness of the memory is palpable in details of novel building processes as well as the adventure and excitement of do-it-yourself construction and living rough.

Home: the word has a similar emotional meaning all over the world, and also a very different one, each country offering its own definitional nuances. The Welsh have their word, *Hiraeth*, and the Welsh writer, Val Bethell, describes it as:

(T)he link with the long-forgotten past, the language of the soul, the call from the inner self. Half forgotten – fraction remembered. It speaks from the rocks, from the earth, from the trees and in the waves. It's always there … There is no comparable word in English; it describes the feeling that true home feels like, wherever.

Hiraeth is not homesickness, exactly, it is more a longing; a deep well of loss for home or what home represents to you. If there is such a word feeling in Yorkshire, its emotional resonance is surely found in a colliery brass band or a Yorkshire accent overheard somewhere far away from the county – that sudden flash of recognition when you hear a ghost speak.

The cry of a peregrine falcon above the moors.

A miner's clogs on cobbles.

The smell of a wet lump of coal.

That is Yorkshire.

And as for Australia? In his study on migration in Australia, Keith Jacobs suggests that all migrant writing can be understood 'as a response to and contemplation on the meaning of home.' The sound of a didgeridoo, a magpie's warble, Peter Allen at the piano singing 'I Still Call Australia Home', the whirr of summer cicadas, the Qantas logo, the easy, friendly, 'G'day'. 'Home can be an amorphous concept,' writes Shelley Hepworth, in her article, 'The Smell of Gum Trees and Rejection: the Australians locked out of "home" by Covid Border Closures.' Hepworth believes we associate home:

with our friends and loved ones, or perhaps the more abstract notion of national identity. But equally home is in the landscapes we have grown to know and love. "Landscape has exerted a kind of force on me that is every bit as geological as family," Tim Winton wrote in his nonfiction book *Island Home* in 2017. "Like many Australians, I feel this tectonic grind – call it familial ache – most keenly when abroad."

These days, home has also taken on a pejorative meaning. 'Going home' suggests being sent back a failure; from the Big Brother house, the competitive kitchen, the room makeover set. Returning means you've failed, and your punishment is a retreat to all you hoped to escape: you have given up your dreams of an old life replaced by one more vivified, or transformed by a very public success. Home then, is also where the dullards go, those who don't have the skills or stamina to succeed. It is cosy, comfortable, but it reeks of a lack of adventure. That's how our family came to see those British who migrated to Australia but decided to return to the UK. They didn't give the place long enough. They weren't prepared to suffer. They had ideas above their station so found life in Australia too classless or brash. They were cowards or *whinging Poms*.

In *On Not Going Home*, James Wood says '…to have a home is to become vulnerable. Not just to the attacks of others, but to our own adventures in alienation.' Once you establish a new home as a migrant you need to begin homebuilding slowly, tentatively, though this depends on how worthy those around you – those gatekeepers who determine who will come to a country and participate in its national narratives – deem your role in the new place.

Home manifests in other ways too: it travels with you like a wraith. Maya Angelou believes that we can never really leave home because we carry 'the shadows, the dream, the fears and dragons of home' under our skin, at the corners of our eyes and 'possibly in the gristle of an earlobe.' Migrants seem to carry their former houses on their bodies, like a tattoo or an architect's blueprint for all future houses. In each line of a floor plan rests a family's ghostly former hearth, the foggy, bacon-scented warmth of the breakfast kitchen, coal tar soap, the lavender brushed against as you open the front door, the flap of freshly-laundered sheets on a clothesline. To keep alive these memories, that former home must be recreated in new ways in a new place, in a new house, a new *home*. The difficulty is getting the balance right, celebrating the new while maintaining the old; not in a maudlin, regretful way, but in a manner that still welcomes the ghosts.

The long sea voyage and the stint with relatives did nothing to disperse the memories of my parents' former homes. They still dreamed of Royston's cellars and coal stores, of horsehair couches and rickety kitchen chairs, of attics and allotments and vegetable plots. Some of these things would make their way into their suburban dreams in Bankstown, where my parents' Yorkshire dreamscape was superimposed onto Bankstown's shire maps and green spaces, onto the area's Wianamatta shale, its clay content perfect for roses. By 1950 they had bought their quarter acre block thanks to the gift of £200 from Aunt Kate in Barnsley. I am named after her, no doubt in gratitude. One day, in this new home, would reside a comfortable, temporal juxtaposition – the past, the present and the future, Yorkshire and Australian interwoven.

The historian Susannah Radstone recalled a friend describing why he couldn't leave his country to migrate to Australia. It was Australia's 'newness', he said, its lack of history and the knowledge that history should rest underfoot in our everyday peregrinations through place. It was what wouldn't be there, under his feet, she writes, that led him to that view:

Beneath the streets of the old world, but missing in Australia, he said, are the vestiges and remains laid down by the centuries; layers that somehow make their presence felt, even if they are glimpsed only rarely, when the streets are dug up. Perplexed, and yet reaching for an explanation about why he felt that these invisible layers were so essential to him, my colleague said that all he knew was that they somehow sustained him and enabled him to live.

As a child I was far more interested in the people who constituted family than my country's history. What surrounded me, what was 'underfoot' meant little at that stage. I watched my parents' ambitions with curiosity; of them, but different. A new home seemed a grand idea. Its newness would transform all of us into suburban Australians – no longer Pommy migrants. I wanted what my Australian friends had – generational connections with place. A new home needed tradition and what better exemplar of that than grandparents. They were the anchors that held a family firmly in place; the sacred repositories of memories, of long-held family traditions and wisdom. I often carefully scrutinised school friends with their grandparents and wondered at the role these elderly relatives played in my friends' lives. They seemed to share all manner of things with grandparents who influenced the ways in which they spoke, or their sense of belonging, especially in schoolyard stories told over lunch or in classroom exercises that drew on family adventures. What did I have in lieu of that?

School friends who came from a long line of Australians often spoke of holidays in the country, when they visited grandparents with farms or homes in beachside towns. Road trips to visit them seemed to pulse with excitement and I listened with interest as they talked about ponies and sheep sheds and orchards full of peach trees or apples. Another friend went each year to relatives who lived in Nambucca Heads, a beachside town in the north of New South Wales. The town's name seemed exotic, as did their mode of transport. The family packed themselves into an old Holden station wagon and headed off, stopping at familiar roadside cafes and service stations for a milkshake or a picnic. As we never had a car, our holidays were necessarily closer to home and ideally to be made in a one-hour train trip. We didn't have relatives to greet us when we got there; those grandparents and aunts and uncles who made my Australian friends' treks seem doubly romantic.

Such are the comforts of a house viewed from a train, a ferry, a childhood memory cast in the return from a day at the seaside. Shrinking, narrowing as the fibro suburbs welcomed us back, the lights switched on, home reclaiming us, melancholy, regretful. We 'travel to the land of Motionless Childhood, motionless in the way all Immemorial things are ...' Gaston Bachelard wrote in *The Poetics of Space*. One day these lights, this childhood will be gone – the hope, the struggle, the wild desire for better things, replaced with middle-aged nostalgia for the ephemera of our first home, the garage. All my houses will lead back to that one. According to Bachelard, 'memories of the outside world will never have the same tonality as those of home, and by recalling these memories, we add to our store of dreams; we are never real historians, but always near poets, and our emotion is perhaps nothing but an expression of a poetry that was lost.'

Poetics also resided in those ancient and wiser people who traversed history like sages from a storybook. Those much missed and mythologised grandparents. That was what we lacked. I was always impressed by the idea of grandparents as kinder, wiser and more lenient representatives of home than my parents, though the tales I'd already heard of mine in England should have warned me this was not always so. A kindly granny would offer sweets and stories by a roaring fire, I decided. She would defend me against parental authority, 'spoil me' in the parlance of the day. My Australian cousins had a grandmother, the mother of my aunts, Margaret and Grace, but she seemed too preoccupied with her own grandchildren, so I never made her my surrogate one. That role fell to my kindly Aunt Margaret who was particularly caring of me as a small child. I wonder now whether that was because my mother was still struggling after my birth with the seismic shocks of migration and a new baby, and my aunt stepped in to help. The neighbour next door to my parents also took a role, making me clothes, taking me for outings, indulging me with gifts and sweets. All this attention must have seemed unfair to my older siblings, themselves in need of some indulgence as they adjusted to a new life in Sydney.

Hiraeth, I have now discovered, may not be an alien word after all, as my family can claim a Welsh connection of sorts. Before they lived in Yorkshire, my maternal grandmother's family came from Wales. She was born there, and only went to Yorkshire as a young woman. Her side of the family came originally from Dorset and no one knows why they moved on to Wales. I only learned of this when I looked into the family history while in Barnsley. I was disappointed at first when I discovered her origins. They didn't fit the family narrative of generational links to Yorkshire, though my affection for the word 'hiraeth' might have had its seeds in place. My grandmother was 'in service' from a young age and when I finally met her, she often spoke about the work she did in a hotel or boarding house in some English seaside town. It never was named. I wondered whether this might be the origin of her children's love of seaside towns. Perhaps she was happiest cleaning and scrubbing to the sounds of the sea.

My enduring image of her though is the old woman standing on the deck of the *Himalaya* when she finally arrived in Sydney. We went on board to collect her once the ship berthed, and I was at last able to see close-up just what a grandparent looked like. I also was able to explore an ocean liner – an ambition of mine since first hearing about the *Empire Brent*. We wandered the *Himalaya's* corridors and dining rooms. Poked our noses into a games room, a bar. Marvelled at the swimming pool and the little shop from which you could buy a celluloid Kewpie doll sailor with *Himalaya* written across his sailor's cap. My grandmother arrived with suitcases and trunks packed with all her things, and it soon became clear she was not intending this to be a short stay. As it turned out, she lived with us for the rest of her life, though she made a further trip home.

Her suitcases were also full of things she had brought as gifts. She'd collected some exotica on her travels to Sydney through the Mediterranean and the Suez Canal as my parents had done, as well as photos and menus and decorations from festive occasions on board the ship – she'd won the Glamorous Granny competition one night. She also brought with her something indomitable. Within months, she had chummed up with my mother's church friends. She was always off on outings with them with her special railway pensioner ticket. She also ventured into places like Lightning Ridge where she went opal digging. Given the stories I'd heard of my bullying grandfather, I'd imagined a downtrodden old lady who needed to live with us because no one else would have her. I learned over the years that followed that she was an adventurer, used to getting her own way. And so she stayed, dominating our lives until her death in 1974.

In *The Poetics of Space*, Gaston Bachelard also reflects on the way time, ambition and memory stalk our ideas of home. 'Sometimes the house of the future is better built, lighter and larger than all the houses of the past, so that the image of the dream house is opposed to that of the childhood home,' he writes:

Maybe it is a good thing for us to keep a few dreams of a house that we shall live in later, always later, so much later, in fact, that we shall not have time to achieve it. For a house that was final, one that stood in symmetrical relation to the house we were born in would lead to thoughts – serious, sad thoughts – and not to dreams. It is better to live in a state of impermanence than one of finality.

After their epic journey, my parents certainly wanted permanence, something my peripatetic meandering has denied me. A permanent new home would represent a vindication of their decision to leave Yorkshire: it would offer a lifestyle that would have eluded them had they stayed put in post-war Britain's austerity and rationing. There would be a plumbed bathroom, three bedrooms, a lounge and kitchen-diner, a huge garden filled with fruit trees and vegetables and flowers. This was the reward at the end of their epic journey, their Ithaca or Eden.

The house they planned was a common bungalow design for the 1950s, hardly big, but big enough for themselves and their kids. I was always surprised when I entered the houses of friends built to the same design. My friends' parents – usually far tidier than mine – made their spaces seem lighter and bigger. I attributed our cramped, messier way of living to my parents' desire – unconscious or deliberate – to recreate something of Yorkshire's clutter in a suburban

Australian space. How else could I explain the dusty, dark interior of the new house other than to locate it within the floor plan of a Yorkshire terrace?

You still see post-war fibro houses like the one my parents built as you drive around Sydney's suburbs, but they are fast dying out. There is a call now to protect them with a heritage listing, as they are being demolished and replaced by rapacious brick two-story mansions; *McMansions*, we call them. These new houses are rewriting an earlier migrant narrative of self-building, community and temporary homes lived in with patience. They speak of ambition and luxury and *en suites* in a way that the modest post-war houses of migrants and working-class battlers never could. Times were tougher then and people's expectations hadn't been shaped by television's obsession with transformation narratives. The repetitive cycle of extensions and renovations and makeovers, for houses to be redesigned and refurbished, over and over again, hadn't dictated the ways in which people lived in their post-war fibro houses in the 1950s and 60s. For people like my parents, money was tight and you made do with what you had. Interiors rarely changed, and when our fibro house was sold after my mother moved into a nursing home, it looked barely different from how it had been in the 1950s and 60s.

'In an old house,' TS Eliot wrote in *The Family Reunion*, 'there is always listening, and more is heard than is spoken':

And what is spoken remains in the room, waiting for the future to hear it.
And whatever happens began in the past, and presses hard on the future.

What then, can be said of a new house?

Without history, a new house is like a stock without flavour. Not cooked enough, not enough ingredients or seasoning. A new house has no longevity and the new paint, the sweet timber smell of freshly cut joists, the chalky white crosses on newly installed windows, speak nothing of history, just hard work. How long does it take for a house to be conferred with history? Generations of new souls are needed. But how many generations? Apart from my father's cousins, my family had no history in Australia. We were a new generation of new Australians, still tethered to the old country. Our house in Bankstown reflected this status. It rose slowly as we kids and our friends played on its foundations and frame, each new stage paid for and quietly celebrated. The scents that accompanied the house's progress were paint, tar, newly sawn wood, varnish. They danced with the heat waves that pulsed from the stacks of terracotta tiles waiting to be fixed to the roof and the cloying scent of newly-planted roses and crab apple blossom. As we played amongst the off cuts of wood and fibro, we remained unaware that the fibro was made of deadly asbestos.

At the peak of Australia's 1950s building boom, writes the National Trust's Carol Roberts in *The Hawkesbury Gazette*:

One third of new homes were constructed of fibro with timber frames and corrugated fibro or iron roofs, but terracotta roof tiles were becoming increasingly popular … With timber strap work covering the joins, fibro was popular for houses, garages, sheds and shops and was painted with Kalsomine in pastel colours of cream, baby blue, green, pink or white. For many the concept of freshly painted white walls with red roof tiles represented an 'overall effect of cleanliness.'

Our house was baby blue.

My mother had grown up in a house in Yorkshire with foundations, and a basement, that stretched back to the times of Henry VIII and the dissolution of the monasteries. It was a house heavy with history; grimy with it, I would discover, when I first stood before it in the 1970s. I thought it was built of black granite, only to discover on a visit decades later, with the house's coal dust and soot removed, that it was built of golden stone. My mother talked of it with a mix of pride and fear. One punishment meted out by her severe father was to be locked in a cellar populated with black beetles, or 'black clocks' as she called them. There were happy memories too, of a patriotic garden bed planted in red, white and blue flowers, the walk to church on Sundays and children's games in the streets. That childhood self in Royston seemed the last thing my mother abandoned, and it arrived back, wraith-like, to possess her dementia-florid, final days in her care home as a childish, giggling girl whose only memories were of the Yorkshire house she'd left behind.

I reflected on this house in Royston as I read John Moseley's poem:

In this house all souls dwell
Those who call
Those who venture
The rooted and the despised
In time and thought
Memory and repentance.

My mother may have ventured to Australia, but something of her remained in her old home in Royston still.

From the late 1940s to the mid-1960s Australia received over 2 million migrants, who, like my parents, had fled Europe after World War II. They had entered a country and a culture that 'was both curiously familiar and disconcertingly strange.' In my class at Condell Park Primary School, I recall only one or two students who were born of Australian parents. In the days before the Australian Labour Party's multiculturalism policies under the leadership of the colourful Minister for Immigration, Al Grassby, most students whose first language wasn't English quickly learned to speak and write it. Others struggled along, under the tutelage of sometimes less-than-patient teachers. Our homes offered insights into each other's cultures and I can still recall the shocked curiosity that comes with a first encounter with cultural difference.

The houses of my school friends from Southern Europe seemed to be sparsely furnished. They had linoleum floors and white walls. They were redolent with the scents of food of which I had no knowledge but know well enough now – spicy sausages, garlic, Parmesan cheese and pasta. The home of a Spanish friend had the added scent-sophistication of her father's Cuban cigars. Embroidered wall hangings adorned the walls of a friend from Lithuania, and I often felt a compulsion to run my hands over their dense and brightly coloured flowers and scrolls. Entering my parents' cluttered house afterwards always felt like a shock. We were different, untidy, and both parents were hoarders – while other friends' families seemed happy to live lean and unencumbered lives. What did I make of it? As a child it confused and surprised me and added to my sense of alienation. Were people from England always messy? Where exactly did our home belong in this cultural diversity? I was never sure.

During the family's last year at my aunt and uncle's house, our temporary house was built, a garage. The garage was tiny, its dimensions allowed by the local council of the time as an emergency dwelling to ease the post-war housing shortage. Many of my friends lived in garages too, and this shared privation went some way towards normalising what it meant to be squashed into a compact space while a proper house was built. We chatted at school about where we slept. We daydreamed about how wonderful our new houses would be and what colour we'd paint our bedrooms. Through my friends' stories, I learned not to feel so badly done by about the long wait for a proper home and the cramped conditions we endured while we waited. As migrants, we were all in this together. Years later, this shared experience was confirmed when I read that between 1949 and the 1960s tens of thousands of new Australians had lived in exactly the same way, working on weekends and spare evenings to build the house of their dreams while saving as much as they could by living in a space barely big enough for a car.

In her doctoral thesis, *Just a Roof Over Their Heads: Temporary Dwellings on Sydney's Urban Fringe 1945 to 1960*, Nicola Pullan writes that 'the most common size recorded for a single garage was 3.6 metres wide by 7.2 metres long, providing enough space to divide into separate sleeping and living quarters.' In our garage's confined space my father soldiered on and my mother gave in to her own homesickness in her quiet, withholding way; just getting on with things, like Dad, but silently. The joy of living as a family, no longer beholden to Uncle Mick's and Aunt Margaret's generosity, was blighted by my parents' first encounter with a dodgy Australian builder who failed to return to fix the garage's leaking roof or replace the windows which were smaller than promised.

It took a long time before this adaptive mode of living made its way into Australia's popular culture. The first I saw of a migrant's garage on film was in the 1984 Australian movie, *Silver City*, directed by Sophia Turkiewicz. This depiction reassured me in some way that our experience in Bankstown was not so limited or shameful after all. The film's Polish characters, new migrants to Australia, lived in a garage just as we had, albeit in a tidier and more organized way. And as I saw in Vietnam a decade later, proud parents could still ensure their children were turned out in neat and clean school uniforms despite the dearth of space in which to wash and iron. I felt ashamed when I first went to Vietnam in the mid-1990s, in part for the role my country had played in the Vietnam War and also because the people I met in Hanoi managed so well during a time of great deprivation – optimistically making do, recycling and rebuilding. I did that thing that is often so much easier to do when closely observing another culture rather than your own. I understood. Through these reflections, the garage gained a new perspective and I ceased to see my memories of it as a burden.

Two adults, three children, one of them a new baby: while we all waited for our house to grow beyond its foundations, its brick pillars offered an eloquent footprint of the rooms-to-be, rising above them airy and invisible, a dream house of skies and clouds and breezes. This interior/exterior, old world/new world duality is reflected in one of my earliest memories, from a day when I stood at the garage's back door and looked out into the garden. The sky was full of birds. Crows, I think, because my memory suggests a slimy blackness of wing; wet, as though the birds had emerged from a river. They might even have been magpies but I don't recall a magpie's flash of white or the marble in the throat warble from a magpie's tilted-back head. No yellow eyes, no sharp orange claws; just that sudden sky-shrug, the air folding and concertinaing around wings and feathers. The pussy willow by the door was a perpendicular intrusion into sky. Silk-worm pupae, torpedo flowers bristling with egg yolk stamen. I knew tiny new green leaves would follow so I must have stood in that doorway a previous spring to watch the tree's progress from nib, to bud, to flower and leaf during a month just like this one of bee-buzzing and birds and the whisper of wind in willow.

I would like to think this was my earliest memory, but these flashes – as potent as black wings and sun on wet black feathers – suggest it wasn't. I was already too familiar with progression by then, through the ways that a memory installs itself, infects and stains. It was raining, and the puddles were textured with raindrops. They doused the reflections of the tree, the birds, the sky, forming a conversation of puddle with rain. The rain on the garage roof almost drowned it out. The air outside was cold, the inside warmer with the heat from the wood-burning stove, so my front was cold and my back quite hot. I was a bifurcated girl; half chilly, half cozy, and I liked the sensation. It was curious. If I turned, I could reverse it, but then I'd lose my command of the scene outside and I did not want to do that.

The garage seemed to be full of shadows and whispers, zones where the real could clash with the imagined. This fusion of the domestic interior and the poetic exterior seemed to capture what the writer, Richard Holmes, has identified as *l'histoire apprise*, or history as it is normally learned and heard, and *l'histoire surprise*, or overheard history. From it, I spun my childhood memories and my understanding of what was happening around me.

Our garage was partitioned into two sections; our parents'

bedroom with their wardrobe forming the wall between the two 'rooms', and the space where we children slept, our beds acting as seating when we weren't sleeping in them. Once electricity had been connected to the garage, we spent most of our time around the kitchen table, listening to the radio. There was the wood-fired stove, and a tap over a sink where we washed; our clothes were scrubbed at a couple of concrete tubs outside. Down the end of a path was the outdoor 'dunny' which was emptied by the night carter every week. The toilet always smelled of phenyl. I have strong memories of this period, a canvas I describe to friends as being like the dark interior paintings Van Gogh created before he discovered sunflowers and sunshine. Blackouts were frequent and we'd sit around an alarming kerosine lamp until power was restored. I remember the strange puffing sound of the lamp and the panic we children felt lest it explode.

A first home is an essential victory in the migrant experience; it is a haven, a place in which to feel safe, to be yourself in a culture in which being yourself may challenge the prevailing culture and add to a sense of difference. As Ghasan Hage writes:

> a home has to be a space open for opportunities and hope. Most theorizations of the home emphasize it as a shelter, but, like a mother's lap, it is only a shelter that we use for rest before springing into action and then return to, to spring into action again. [...] A home has to be an existential launching pad for the self. [...] It has to be open enough that one can perceive opportunities of "a better life": the opportunity to develop certain capacities and skills, the opportunity of personal growth, and, more generally, the availability of opportunities for "advancement"

whether as upward social mobility or emotional growth or in the form of accumulation of symbolic or monetary capital.

As our house took shape, my parents continued to extend and set out their garden. Fruit trees, vines, vegetable patches, hedges and shrubs and the first of the hundreds of rose bushes that would be supplemented each parental birthday and Christmas until the garden was bulldozed by the house's new owners in 2007. This garden soothed and healed. It was as if a family allotment in Yorkshire had expanded into every gardener's dream of vast riches of fruit and vegetables, fertile soil, sunshine and gentle rain, and taken root in Sydney. The garden provided bounty as well as a sense of ownership in ways the fledgling house just couldn't. Permanence for both my parents always came in the form of planted things that took root, flowered, bore fruit, offered shade and mulch. They were always happiest in the garden.

Our Italian neighbours were doing the same, as were the Greeks, Lithuanians, Spaniards and Croatians. In each of their gardens, the produce varied, their quarter acre blocks offering the tastes of home. We had our specific rituals too – there was no 'chippy' on the corner as there had been in Royston, so we picked our tomatoes and doused them in vinegar, salt and pepper, wrapped them in greaseproof paper and jokingly called them 'fish and chips.' We harvested strawberries and runner beans and, when the trees were larger and fruiting, our mouths turned purple with the mulberries and plums we devoured as we ran around under them, barefooted and suntanned. My father experimented with foods he'd never tasted, like chokos, guavas and native rosellas for making jam. He was disappointed with his eggplants because they didn't taste like eggs.

Was there a shared Australian dream? Did we all work towards something intrinsic to our nation as new Americans are expected to do? The Sydney in which I grew up seemed to hold home ownership as its goal. As soon as you could, you built or bought a house. Having your own home tethered you to place. It liberated you from avaricious landlords or social housing waiting lists. It was a source of great pride to write home to relatives that the house would be paid off in however many years. It is no accident that we children were posed in front of the house as our parents built it, step by step, our heights and physiques growing as the house grew. Real estate still shapes Sydney's sense of itself and it is a common joke that no Sydney dinner party ever avoids some discussion about house prices and the best suburbs in which to live. I suspect this narrative was born of that postwar experience. You arrive. You save. You build a house. Your children grow up and buy a house too. The houses appreciate in value, adding generational riches. With soaring house prices in all of Australia's cities these days, that dream no longer exists.

As I looked for a house in Liverpool, accompanied by my middle-class fantasies of fireplaces, white walls, high ceilings, bookcases and Persian rugs, I could see how large their planned new Australian house must have seemed to my parents after the tiny two-up, two-down back-to-backs of England's industrial north. I wanted to settle in Liverpool as quickly as possible and to do that I needed a permanent address, one to which I could invite new friends to dinner and establish a study lined with bookcases and books. An old house, one with history, was an important factor in my search. How else might I fit into a city filled with some of Britain's most impressive Georgian streetscapes, and a docklands area that once drew migrants and shipping from all parts of the world? My Australian childhood had been spent creating a new house in a new place. It is no accident, then, that in this old/new place, Liverpool, I live in a house that is more than 200 years old.

The key to my parents' sense of alienation rested in their 'newness', their lives now lived as a series of new experiences with no connecting tissue to the old life. I watched them cling to their Yorkshire identities all their lives and I often found myself wondering about the success of migration, the inevitable question being 'was all that upheaval worth it?' They had survived the blitz and the cataclysms of World War II, and no one had been pursing them with guns or bombs in peaceful, post-war Britain. Their lives were not at risk. How might they have lived had their home been in Yorkshire? The same way, or differently? Even today, when I watch historical British television or films, especially those set just after the war and in the 1950s, I often find myself locating our family in the scenes – the London smog, the great snowy winters, rationing, the Queen's coronation, the Suez crisis. We'd missed them all and with them the sense of belonging that came with the community flag waving celebrations at trestle tables, the worried huddles around radios or televisions, the patient shop queues of rationing, the snow shovelling. What would our house have been like in one of those bunting-strung Yorkshire streets?

I realize now that a bungalow in Australia can easily mimic the interiors of a Yorkshire terrace. On my first visit to Yorkshire, by then a fan of modern, Danish styling, I was struck by the ways in which the English houses of my relatives were often over-decorated and chintzy. Overly-large furniture or ornaments and cushions dominated small rooms. People seemed to live on top of one another.

The scent of the meals they ate lingered for days. Coal fires spat in narrow, warmth-defying grates. There was something fusty about those houses too; a tincture of old lady, chocolate biscuits and coal tar soap. My relatives seemed not to notice any of this. Their houses were welcoming and they were happy, but I found myself wanting to go for long walks in the fresh air to get away from them. As I walked, I realized I was witnessing a simulacrum: the houses reminded me of my parents' perfect recreation in Australia, and especially their first home in the garage.

Despite the dark memories, I sometimes wish I could go back to the garage's confined space one more time, in part because I suspect it would allow me to better understand how its pernicious smallness shaped who I became. It was a crow draped over my shoulders; sinister, black, anxious, and I have spent a lifetime prising it off and casting it aside. But I also need to be in that space to appreciate how a sense of ourselves is shaped, just as the church shaped priests and nuns into gothic arches of self-contained prayer and contemplative shuffle. I think too of prisoners who develop agoraphobia if left in the gaol's exercise yard too long and grow needy for the narrow four walls of their cells.

Our garage was a dark space in a world that was all light and shade, the garden outside already flowering with my parents' prize dahlias and roses. In and out; the inner to be avoided until there was no choice but to re-enter its crowded gloom. I recall the radio plays, comedy hours and quiz shows that brought some much-needed mirth into the space. A big stove, a sink, beds, curtains, toys too, and books certainly – we were all avid readers. And what did we read? Stories about England and English children who taunted us from the books' pages, from armchairs in front of crackling fires, from History with a capital H that sneered, *look what you're missing*. This only would change when I went to school, and I moved from the narratives of lakes and moors and boarding schools in England to stories of the Australian bush.

It was when I was introduced to the novels of contemporary Australian children's writers like Ivan Southall and Nan Chauncey, via the Education Department's school magazine or the radio classes we listened to in stuffy, hot classrooms, our heads on our hands, that I began to extricate myself from the trap of my parents' England and its houses. Bankstown and Condell Park Primary School took on a different light; real adventures might even happen there. Those Australian children's books prompted a forage through the Bankstown library with a more nationalistic fervour. I read the fore-mentioned, plus Ethel Turner and Elyne Mitchell, and developed an affinity with the Australian bush, for Australian bush houses with corrugated iron roofs and wide verandas, for wire doors that slapped shut as a child ran, barefooted, onto sun-brittle buffalo grass. My conversion to rough-and-tumble fictional Australian children and their Aussie houses, unconstrained by the ties of Empire and social class, seemed at first disloyal. Not only was I being unfaithful to my parents' carefully packed *Golden Treasury* and books from their own childhoods, but to English authors as a whole and their boarding school midnight feasts of buttery crumpets and trips to London to see the ballet, or wet caravan holidays in Wales. The ruggedness of setting and character in Australian stories seemed to galvanise my limbs; from then on, there was no more wistful reading about England. I had my own country to explore.

As a teenager, though, I garnered less comfort from my nationalism. Instead, I found myself resenting those early, contained years. I harboured the view that the garage had played a key role in my emotional development, and it was not a happy one. I was like a crab; the garage a glued-on, burdensome shell. It had thwarted my confidence, made me susceptible to dark moods or stubbornness – or so I decided. I would spend much of my adult life escaping the memory of the garage's confines through travel, study, work and writing, or through buying increasingly-prosperous houses in gentrified inner-city Australian suburbs. How else could I account for the obsessional desire for large, clean rooms flooded with sunlight?

My father also told stories of other houses, of course, those in England he still missed; of his childhood games, when a lump of slag from the pit could be thrown at a tin bath hanging on the side of someone else's house to make a mighty clatter and send the house's owner roaring after him. He told these stories with relish, and – I now realise – relief, not nostalgia. He was grateful that in Australia we no longer had to live like that. Listening to them, or looking at photos of Liverpool, Manchester or Leeds taken in the 1950s, 1960s and 1970s, the poor in squalid rooms with damp and peeling walls, I came to compare our lives in the garage favourably after all. It was only temporary. We ate well, we were clean and well-dressed, we had a huge garden in which to play and it rewarded us with its fruit and vegetables. In a period of post-war prosperity and full employment, my father had a job. If we ever sounded resentful or complained about what other children had, my parents' stories took on the moralising tones of the Sunday school sermons we endured every Sunday and where even our hymns, 'The wise man built his house upon the rock …', seemed to promote home ownership. Our parents had come to Australia for a better life for us kids and we should be grateful that they had.

My parents also wrote letters home extolling the joys of their new life. There is testament to this boasting in photos of the house slowly rising; from foundations, to frame, to fibro cladding. We children stand self-consciously behind huge baskets of tomatoes, plums and grapes in those show-off photos, chosen to present the bounty from the sunny exterior fecundity of our garden life, rather than the cramped and dark interior world of the garage. Did these photos help to 'facilitate a connection between two histories, two worlds, complicit yet also distinct' as George Kouvaros has claimed? Anyone in England viewing my mother or the lanky and tanned children posed behind piles of fruit must have seen us as mythological in our luck. The duality is unmistakable though – external prosperity, internal privation. The price paid for our house, our reward, was hard work, patience and a constant pushing aside of any regrets.

One of the first things my father built on our block of land was a letter box, a neat tin affair with a sloping lid that made it look like a little tin house on top of a post, or like one of my brother's Hornby tin train stations. The number 80 was painted clumsily on the front. It waited daily for the postman, who rode on his bike down the hill to our place, to deposit whatever thin aerogramme he had in his mail pouch that day. Sometimes he brought a parcel wrapped in canvas or parachute silk, but as time progressed these thinned out to birthdays and Christmas.

Most parcels arrived just before Christmas, when the air pulsed with cicadas and the acrid scent of privet flowers. Eventually the senders would decide we were too grown up to continue to receive gifts, and just too far away; but while the bounty lasted it acted like a rope, sustaining, supporting, drawing us back to England. The parcels filled the gaps in our memories with little prompts of sweets, like sticks of rock holding inside their sticky circular hardness the names 'Blackpool' or 'Skegness', along with holiday souvenirs from Butlin's camps, hair slides, soap and photographs by the dozen of the life in England we'd missed. English life seemed to be growing more prosperous than ours, an economic phenomenon that flummoxed us all. Hadn't my family travelled all the way to Australia to enjoy greater economic opportunities and prosperity than the families they'd left behind?

This sense of turnabout, of being conned, affected me every time one of the parcels arrived. The gifts inside seemed more sophisticated, more resonant with tradition, than anything we could buy in Bankstown. The English women's magazines my mother devoured contained advertisements for foods like Birds Trifle, a complex layering of custard and fruit and cream that I imagined was eaten from cut glass bowls in a garden in which blackbirds trilled. Viewed in the sweltering heat of a Sydney summer, the Christmas beetles concussing themselves against our new fly screens, it felt as though our voluntary exile had been paid for with the loss of tradition and Birds custard and family, and a house that was taking far too long to finish.

This experience of brand nostalgia is common to the children of the colonies and also to the children of emigrants who have been 'colonised' in their own way by their parents' nostalgic memories. Trinidadian writer V.S. Naipaul remembered 'the Penguin paperbacks which contained advertisements for certain British things – chocolates, shoes, shaving cream.' When Naipaul arrived in London, he discovered that these British things, though still advertised in Trinidad, no longer existed, or existed only as redundant advertisements in British magazines.

The letters sent to my parents were read and reread, the paper browning and crisping as though the hands that held them were aflame. Brown at the edges, the neat blue ink lines to be savoured again when we kids had gone to school or bed, or after work when my father had changed into his gardening overalls, sat on a makeshift garden bench under the young plum trees and read. Both parents cried. I watched them with the callous curiosity of the future writer. Heads down, bent low over the words. The silent shudder of deep emotion, making sure their tears didn't cause the ink to run. I watched my mother weep over the letter telling her that her father had died and I wrote on a scrap of paper with the cruel heart of a child, 'my mother is a cry baby.'

I have talked to other first-generation Australian writers about their bifurcations; their loyalty to parents who needed to 're-home' the old ways and their children's needs to be fully of their new place. After all, we children were born in it – we didn't migrate to it. It felt like a shameful disloyalty once, when I came upon a picture of the Queen that my mother had helped me stick into my school exercise book. For homework, my class had been asked to create a few pages about where we'd all come from and by 'we' it was clear our parents were included. My friends had drawn maps of the Ukraine, Lithuania, Yugoslavia, Italy, Czechoslovakia or Spain, and sitting at our kitchen table I had drawn a map of England and had placed the picture of the Queen at its centre. My mother had cut the Queen from a *Woman's Own* magazine, and we'd stuck her on with a swipe of Clag glue. The Queen had come unstuck and had fallen out unnoticed by me. I discovered her at recess when I saw her tiny, regal face on the scuffed asphalt that constituted our playground. It wasn't the Queen I saw abandoned there, though; it was my mother and her still raw homesickness and I felt deeply sorry for her, shame too, that I had let her fall so easily onto the ground.

There comes a time when it is too late to go back. For my family, I like to speculate, we reached the crossroads when we moved into our new house and then, three years later, my younger sister was born. One Australian child might put a strain on the link to the old country, but two caused it to break. I barely remember our entry into the new house; it is a memory only in pieces, a kaleidoscope of sensations, scents, touch, sounds. We still sat around the radio at the same old kitchen table, but soon that table was replaced by a laminate and chrome one. We still made use of gifts and recycled second-hand pieces, but these were soon joined by a rented television and new rugs. The space that had seemed so much bigger than the garage soon filled and contracted. The new baby was accommodated in our parents' bedroom, and when our grandmother arrived from the UK this became a permanent sleeping arrangement.

Our house is still there, one of that dying breed of post-war fibro houses, built by migrants who had never built houses before but somehow harnessed the skills to build one in Australia by drawing on friends for whom the favour would be returned as they built their own houses. In my parents' case, this meant the friends they'd made on the *Empire Brent*, the Shaws and Tweedales. As children, we weren't encouraged to be ambitious. University was seen as beyond working class people like us. Any aspirations our parents might have had for themselves seemed to have burned out with their migration and the establishment of a new home – surely their great trip across the oceans, their building of a house and garden, two new Australian children and a new job were enough?

The house lingers in us all, though. It aspired to roses and the thrift of making do, those perversities of expectation where a house became the inanimate representation of what our parents' long sea voyage really had been about – a nice home on a quarter acre block halfway across the world, the mortgage paid off as quickly as possible. Thus, we return to our childhood home through memory, our world shrinking, receding as nostalgia claims us. We return to Bachelard's world of 'motionless childhood … motionless in the way all Immemorial things are.' Our childhood homes gone, all the hopes and struggles of building a new home in a new place are replaced with a middle-aged nostalgia for the childhood homes we left. 'Memories of the outside world will never have the same tonality of those at home,' Bachelard said.

Our family home in Bankstown also retains a tyranny of memory. Now both parents are dead, my siblings and I rarely talk about the house, nor about those unsettled early years when we became Australians, in theory at least. The house might rise before us when a memory needs verification. Was it then? Where was that? Waiting for older siblings' memories to act as the binding agent for something not quite formed. Our parents can't be asked at all. But the dead speak through photographs and tape recordings, in a flickering family home movie of us all standing self-consciously in front of the flowering jacaranda opposite the back door, its bell flowers drifting above us like purple snow.

In 2011 the house my parents built in Bankstown was sold. Each of us kids reacted differently to its sale. We were an amalgam of our adult selves and our childhood ones as we packed up my mother's things; emotionally raw, in grief and denial. Like the photographer, Aram Balakjian, who was floored by 'emotional grenades' as he emptied his family home, we moved between memory, laughter and sadness. Balakjian reflected:

these things that meant so much to someone who meant so much to you … You're dismantling their lives. It's the end of their story. You really have this sense of what's left after we die. Just a bunch of things, really.

As it was prepared for sale, our childhood house was like a magnet, drawing us into its emptiness, its tidiness and preparedness for its new owners while throwing a shadow, an echo of clutter and memories. The experience of the auction was emotionally exhausting. There was grief, confusion, abstraction, anger, all of it derived from seeing the house through a real estate agent's eyes. Our memories were slowly occluded as the house was redefined. Our bedrooms, the marks on the doorframe to show how much we'd grown, the old copper in the laundry, the scent of roses through the open back door. As we ticked off all that needed to be done prior to sale, we might as well have been autopsying a corpse.

We spread out boxes of papers, jewellery and china on the kitchen table. There were shaving mugs featuring the likeness of King George VI and the Queen Mother, a few necklaces and gold rings that had travelled to Australia with my mother. Books that had crossed the ocean with our parents were distributed to the bookish amongst us. The photo box was set aside, and those mysterious children and soldiers frozen in time now reside with my sister. This process of sorting was tinged with regret. We were sad to be selling a house that had been witness to our resettlement and struggle and in which all of us had sacrificed some small part of ourselves. The child standing at the door of the garage, the boy spread out on the floor with his train tracks and Hornby trains, the toddler who gave up her bedroom for her grandmother. The objects we passed around seemed talismans of that story. I would not have been surprised if a touch had set them aglow. They reside now in our various lives, some cherished, some devoid of whatever magic they once held, of no interest to the new generation, awaiting the day when their superfluity gains its own power and the object is sent off to a charity shop.

Writing in the Smithsonian Magazine, Verlyn Klinkenborg describes this kind of abstraction as the way our home aligns everything around us. 'Perhaps you remember a moment,' she writes:

> coming home from a trip, when the house you call home looked, for a moment, like just another house on a street full of houses. For a fraction of a second, you could see your home as a stranger might see it. But then the illusion faded and your house became home again. That, I think, is one of the most basic meanings of home – a place we can never see with a stranger's eyes for more than a moment … When my father died, my brothers and sisters and I went back to his house, where he'd lived alone. It wasn't only his absence we felt. It was as though something had vanished from every object in the house. They had, in fact, become merely objects. The person whose heart and mind could bind them into a single thing – a home – had gone.

One day the house my parents built with so much post-war ambition will be demolished, as have many of the fibro houses around it, and it will be replaced with a far larger, more impressive brick construction to house a new family. In the meantime, it stands as a testament to migration, a palimpsest of hope and optimism overwriting the landscape of Bankstown. As such, it is also a condemnation of our current migration policies, especially those towards refugees who dream of a safe home. Our house was put together by migrants who contributed to Australia's prosperity and development. Post-war Australia was built by people who lived in houses like these. Handing it over to newer migrants seemed a fitting reminder of this role.

Aram Balakjian felt this sense of torch-passing too. His family was 'actually really happy to hand the house over to a new family ... I felt we'd borrowed this space for 30 years. We built these amazing things, and now it was time for someone else to come in.'

Today a Muslim family lives in our house. I have no idea which country they're from, but in our former space they are weaving their own stories, part of their new country, part of their old. These new owners dream *their* dreams, in the house my parents built.

CHAPTER FOUR
Becoming Australian

In 2003 when I was living in Paris on a writer's residency at the Cite Internationale des Arts, I went to the greenhouse in the Jardin des Plantes. The sharp nip of winter was in the air and I was feeling, not homesick exactly, but in need of cultural reminders, a little jolt of something from home – a scent, a touch, a sound. A few days earlier, I had watched the wallabies in the Jardin's zoo with the keen interest with which an expatriate often watches an animal indigenous to their home country. How did they get *here*? I wondered, though I could have been posing that question to myself. For all I knew, those wallabies had been born in France but they still seemed very Australian and out of place, exotic as they nibbled on the neatly-clipped French grass. There was something comical about them too. They were cute, *mignon*, and a long way from their cultural home.

I have felt this mix of displacement and humour when looking at kangaroos or cockatoos in other zoos. Through their bars, they speak of something that binds us to a place, a genetic fingerprint of scents and plants and soil and water. Birds seem to be particularly emblematic of nation – magpies, kookaburras, cockatoos. 'There's this feral flock of cockatoos in my neighbourhood and, when I hear them, I run to the back window of this flat in the hope of catching a glimpse of them,' one expat wrote from Hong Kong. 'They make me feel comforted because they remind me of home.' For another, it's the birdsong … 'The minute you call somebody in Australia, there's some kind of bird in the background of the call, and that makes me very nostalgic.'

I respond in the same way to budgerigars in cages here in England. They have been turned into clowns or parodies of themselves and I imagine them nattering away to their alien English family in a regional UK accent, the theme from *Coronation Street* or *Hollyoaks* playing on the television. Could they ever imagine being at home in the Australian outback? In flight in the wild, a yellow and green and blue wave of screeching movement, thousands of them turning the hot blue sky aflutter, or a slash of colour along the white branches of a ghost gum.

The Jardin des Plantes' greenhouse was full of plants needing air far warmer than the autumn chill outside, and amongst the ferns and bromeliads and creepers was a eucalyptus that exuded the pungent aroma of the Australian bush. I broke off a leaf and I crumpled it into my hands and held it to my nose and took a deep breath. In Proust's city, the gesture seemed reverential, to his madeleines and lime flower tea certainly, but also to my own emotional Australian history. With those indrawn eucalyptus breaths, I was back in a childhood of bushwalks and school campfires, of damper and Billy tea, of huge leafy back gardens and the noisy birds that inhabit an Australian tree's branches; magpies, currawongs, kookaburras, native mynahs. In that moment my homesickness took me somewhere fugal; a rush, a wing-beat, a smell so intense it was primal. I sat in the greenhouse's humid pretence of home and wove my memories of Australia into my own form of keening.

Migrants and expatriates seem to be ambushed by experiences like this repeatedly. I doubt there has ever been a way to resist them. In his essay 'Avoiding it: Writing fiction about place without writing about it,' the Australian writer, Rhett Davis, describes a similar experience to mine, his in London's Kew Gardens. Two years after he had arrived in

London Davis spied a eucalyptus tree in the gardens. It was the smell of it, he wrote:

> its skinny, graceless arms, the way it disturbs the earth. It doesn't belong in this cold, damp soil, under this drab sky. It belongs to hard dirt and scrub, to brilliant blue skies and fierce southern oceans. I don't care what Samuel Johnson said. I'm tired of London, and that doesn't mean shit.

In Liverpool I have been lassoed by an Australian accent and pulled along behind it through a crowd. By a sudden craving for the taste of Vegemite. By the longing for a hot Sunday evening at Nielsen Park, a glass of wine in my hand as I watch the setting sun bronze the harbour, then sink behind the Sydney Harbour Bridge. These moments of national need have been so intense and teetering they might as well have been experienced at the edge of a cliff. A tiny step forward and I would plunge into them. A nostalgia, a need, overwhelming and destabilizing, whispers in your ear – 'wherever you are, wherever you go, however much you experience or change, you are Australian.'

What then does it mean to be an Australian? The question is almost Sisyphean. Just as you think you've reached an answer it rolls away from you again. This question was repeatedly put to us as children by schoolteachers eager to assess how well the migrant kids in my class had assimilated. I'm sure it's still asked at Australia's citizenship ceremonies. The question is further complicated by Australia's diversity. We are a mixed and multicultural nation – how could just one definition suffice? 'The majority of Australians today have a direct personal or parental knowledge of the experiences of migration from more than 100 different cultures and countries of origin,' write Darian-Smith and Hamilton. 'This is evident in a plethora of everyday ways, from the linguistic and belief systems practised in diasporic communities through to the emergences of cross-cultural forms, such as fusion cooking, that are often celebrated as successful and distinctive outcomes of a multicultural Australia.'

As children, we drew maps of Australia and coloured them in – the blue of the sea, the green of the coast, the yellow of the wheat and sheep belt, the red of the Centre. I've spent a lifetime answering the question of national identity in one form or another, from those coloured-in maps, to schoolroom debates, or tipsy barbeques at which my friends and I compared the merits of an Australian wine with one from France or Chile. From all those debates and disagreements I've decided that Australians are chameleons. We adapt, change shape and colour as needed. We hide our backgrounds under a construct of classlessness, flummoxing those for whom class and background matter.

It is partly the accent; that flat, standardized voice that doesn't give much away. Instead of denoting your regional origins, wealth or a private school education as accent does so readily in England, it speaks to non-Australians of beaches and a vast, red outback. Whether we are wealthy or poor, we probably barbeque, enjoy football or cricket and long summery Christmas holidays. We are self-effacing. Enjoy a blue joke. We are a blokey nation; open, friendly. Mates. Some of our finest heroes are the Anzacs, the acronym for Australian and New Zealand Army Corps but now in common use to denote Australianness, or film stars like Errol Flynn, Chips Rafferty, Bryan Brown or Hugh Jackman. Our contemporary female heroes offer a different story. Unlike the drover's wives of Australia's colonial narratives, they are the fair-skinned, elegant few who have escaped to fame elsewhere – more hybrid, really, more American or

British. Actors like Cate Blanchett, Nicole Kidman and Judy Davis learned early to lose their Australian qualities, become more universal, to not play up an 'Aussieness' that their male counterparts are free to indulge. The rest of us women are 'Sheilas'; sun-brown and assertive, we take no prisoners, and all of us, men or women, are presumed to be a bit uncouth and not that sophisticated. We are suspicious of the overly intellectual. We don't like the boastful or 'wankers'. We exude confidence and are suspicious of emotion or people who think too deeply.

Australians are also great travellers, and many have been quick to escape Australia's intellectual constraints, especially the moribund years before the election of Gough Whitlam's government and its support for the arts. Barry Humphries, Robert Hughes, Germaine Greer, Clive James. All escaped. The expatriate Australian writer, Randolph Stowe, thought life in Australia was 'very like being on a cruise ship, living comfortably in good weather with boring company and no particular destination.' Stowe, who spent most of his adult life in Suffolk, England, could have been answering the ubiquitous question of Australianness when he commented that visitors to Australia are struck by the solidity of the Australian character, its lack of doubts.

This search for a neat national identity involves stereotypical nonsense, of course, crafted through characters like Barry Humphries's Dame Edna Everidge or Paul Hogan's Crocodile Dundee. There is no denying that our films, from *They're a Weird Mob* to *Kenny*, often speak of an indestructible quality, a humour that overrides or ignores the more dangerous aspects of racism, migration, class and inequality that are major elements of our history and culture. Australia is also far more complex and diverse than people expect. It is an ancient place and has millennia of indigenous history.

It rankles when people speak of Australia as a new country or part of the 'new' world. That is a colonial construct about who 'discovered' the place, denying its original people their land and culture – the oldest continuous surviving culture in the world – asserting that the continent was empty. In fact, we live on a thin veneer of history, a 'relatively short span of Australia's British settler colonial history, a history that has barely scratched the land's surface.'

Like Australia's vast landscape, our national identity seems to need a particular perspective, as though being viewed from a great height. A humbling is needed, a miniaturisation to neutralize nationalism. In his poem, 'Australia', the late Australian poet, AD Hope referred to Australia as being:

Without songs, architecture, history:
The emotions and superstitions of younger lands
Her rivers of water drown among inland sands,
The river of her immense stupidity.
Whose boast is not: 'we live' but 'we survive'.
A type who will inhabit the dying earth.

The foundations of our nation are shaky, the Australian poet John Kinsella says. 'To include is to exclude, to attempt to define is to imprison and usurp content ... an agenda comes into play ... a value-adding fetishization of landscape to suit a particular end.'

Australia is also multicultural and has been for centuries, from the earliest Indonesians and Chinese and Afghans, the Europeans and Islanders, the Irish and African and American. In the days when people were more freely able to move between countries, drawn by goldfields or pastures, business opportunities or safety, people came to Australia to make their fortunes or find sanctuary. The country has a penal and punishing history that dogs us still, from the convict First Fleet, the genocidal acts against Aboriginal people and their forced removal from their lands, the 'black-birding' or kidnapping of Pacific Islanders to be enslaved workers in our sugar cane fields, to its present-day offshore detention of refugees. For almost a century, we had one of the world's most racist migration policies, the 'White Australia Policy'. It shaped immigration by excluding people from a wide range of countries, privileging the 'whites' from Britain and northern Europe, determining a culture based on skin colour and background that would change only in the late 1960s and with the reforms of Gough Whitlam's Labour government of 1972-75. This is the real Australian history – indigenous, racist, multicultural, reformist, artistic, entrepreneurial and complex.

Over the past 50 years, the hegemony of Australia's whiteness has been challenged potently in the recognition of indigenous land rights, the recognition of prior indigenous ownership and native title rights through the Mabo decision of 1982, and the expression of indigenous culture through art, performance, music and dance.

Migrants also have claimed their place in Australia's narratives, often satirically. In 1994, for example, the artist Hou Leong tackled Australia's cultural stereotyping in a series of photographs which parody mainstream images of Australian identity such as those of Crocodile Dundee. In his work, Leong:

> digitally inserted himself into the picture in order to draw attention to the absence of Asian representations within mainstream images of Australian identity. [...] Although (his) work has a playful aspect, it also speaks to a real

confusion and concerns shared by many Asian-Australians stemming from the disjuncture between their everyday lives – where faces on the street show people of myriad descent, not just Anglo-Australians, versus mainstream media, public culture and even political representation, which construct Australia as almost entirely a constituency of Anglo-Australians.

There have been multiple attempts since to define the Australian character in other ways, such as the opening of the 2000 Sydney Olympic Games in which, inexplicably, squatters on horseback entered the ceremony in advance of the Aboriginal people as though landowners/squatters had a greater claim on the place. None of these is more celebratory of colonialism and land theft than those of Australia Day, celebrated on the 26th of January each year. Our indigenous people mourn it as Invasion Day.

There is always an attempt to engage migrants in the Australia Day narrative. On Australia Day in 2018, for example, the Special Broadcasting Service asked its Hindi listeners what being Australian meant to them. A small business owner from Adelaide, Virendranathi Tripathi, responded: 'Being Australian means: believing in a multi-cultural society that embraces people from all ethnicities (regardless of their faith, culture, race, and skin colour), freedom with responsibility, being inclusive, egalitarian spirit and fair-go.' Virendranath also believed that being Australian meant 'having compassion, tolerance and mutual respect ... being passionate about natural resources and the sports.' For Virendranath, above all, being Australian is 'being a responsible human in One World Family.'

Others have spoken less optimistically about the discrimination they have faced, especially older migrants battling language barriers, fighting for recognition of their qualifications, learning new business practices, experiencing racism and alienation. The Australian migrant experience seems to have been mediated through trials such as these and none has been more repressive than those faced by refugees in Australia's detention centres. Historian Peter Sahlins sees these swings in identity as a 'socially constructed and continuous process of defining friend and enemy.' National identities, he says, 'do not depend on the existence of any objective or cultural differentiation but on the subjective experience of difference.' National identities also contain agonizing constraints. We easily become locked into a culture, Marc Auge says, and only through knowing the merits of another culture do we put our own into perspective.

I doubt that any of these questions of identity concerned my parents as they prepared to leave the UK. They had been attracted to Australia because it was British and they had relatives in Sydney, but they could not have escaped the knowledge that they were privileged by a culture and language that were English. All the posters and recruitment brochures had reassured them they would feel right at home amongst people like themselves. They must have felt doubly reassured as they settled amongst the Bankstown community. Neighbours and relatives were British-born or British by descent, and most non-English-speaking 'new Australians' from Europe kept to their own friendship groups. I don't think my parents ever imagined Australia as anything other than somewhere familiar, but there is a certain irony about the way in which they left a home where they seemed to live on the periphery of a wider England.

Just how British were they? They knew nothing of England outside Yorkshire, except through the films and newsreels they watched in the cinema in Barnsley or news and plays they heard on the radio. That other England was found in London or the Home Counties, not Yorkshire. Given they knew nothing about their own homeland, what could Australia offer by way of dreamscapes and fantasies? Was it something imagined, something hoped for, a Britishness from a Britain they had never seen?

In a *Guardian* article, 'Why it's time to stop talking about English Identity,' the journalist Alex Niven wrote:

> The historian Benedict Anderson famously argued that all countries are 'imagined communities' that develop their own fictional narratives over the years to create a sense of shared belonging. But in England's case, because it has not been an actual nation state since at least as far back as the Act of Union with Scotland in 1707, its national community is more imaginary than usual.

I see in my parents' migration all the complexities of place and identity that the Australian historians, Sara Wills and Kate Darian-Smith, have identified as 'the complex transitional narratives of migrancy, ethnicity, and "belonging" among British migrants in modern Australia.' By migrating, my parents had decided that Australia was a country that would provide a new way to live. No coal mines, no strikes or economic uncertainty, no rain, no rationing, no fog or snow. It would be a Technicolor place, bright with opportunity. They would soon discover that most of the things they were fleeing were to be found in their new home also.

There were times too when the Australian landscape flummoxed them, and they found it hard to feel the beauty in it. It would take my mother almost her entire lifetime to concede that the Blue Mountains or Sydney's

Royal National Park had a particular, rugged beauty. She never felt comfortable in such a wild landscape and usually spent visits in a café or kiosk gazing out at it over a cup of steaming tea. She wasn't alone in this sense of alienation. Quoted in Hammerton's and Thomson's *Ten Pound Poms*, a new British migrant in Hobart wrote of her new city:

> I didn't find it beautiful. I found it threatening. The mountain rose menacingly above the Hill's hoist. The land had no history that I could read from it. Everything looked untended, shabby, peeling, dry and horribly powerful as though the bush or the sea might suddenly rise up and casually flatten all the little wooden houses. And here too was the misery of the loss of the known, not of network and ritual but of familiar places and the sense of possession that familiarity bestows. Later I felt unhappy that I couldn't, without resorting to books, open the landscape for my children as my mother had opened Gloucestershire for me.

The unexplored dream England that accompanied my parents would be a useful companion too, a touchstone for all the values they wanted in their new place. England in Australia. No wonder they so assertively held onto their lost Yorkshire; it was like holding onto a necessary and ancient myth. There was an irony in all this too. They couldn't talk about London or other places in England with us – these places were discovered together as a family through English magazines and newsreel footage, and later from the postcards we children sent to our parents from our own visits to England. But they could share Yorkshire and that is exactly what they did, mapping it, narrating it, turning it into our own dream country – mythical, imagined and real – to be visited one day in a kind of reverse pilgrimage.

As was the case for most migrants who made such an epic decision, the family mantra about why they had migrated always was 'we did it so you could have a better life.' The truth of that is debatable but one thing was certain: in travelling to Australia my parents gifted me and my siblings a healthy and outdoor way in which to live. Ours was an Australian childhood spent in the sunshine. Outdoors. Chasing balls along beaches, tanning on multi-coloured beach towels, the roar of the sea pierced by the shrill calls of seagulls and children throwing a stick for a dog or packing sand into sandcastles. My parents rarely joined us on the sand. Their role was as observers only, minding a picnic table under the Norfolk pines. I imagine they may have spoken quietly to one another about how lucky we were, or how they had made the right decision. There they sat like two rigid figures in a sepia photograph from a long time ago; shadow people, hesitant beach goers. They had sacrificed their old lives for their children. In and out of the sun we flashed like the golden carp in some Chinese pond. Out of place and time, our parents seemed happy enough in their chosen space with their sun hats on, minding the packed sandwiches, thermos of tea and plastic bottle full of frozen orange cordial for the kids. I doubt they ever envied those parents who swam or kicked at the frill of waves at the sea edge with their children; the Speedo-clad, bronzed Aussie parents with their sand-dusted picnics and Eskies under beach umbrellas.

My parents' caution may have been justified. Both were very fair skinned, and had been caught out a couple of times by sunburn so bad they were debilitated by it for days. My father had once gone fishing with my brother on Tuggerah Lake, unaware that the skin behind the knees was vulnerable to the rays of the sun reflected off water on the floor of the boat. So bad was his sunburn, he couldn't straighten his legs for days afterwards: he walked bent over, crab-like and cursing. So, in the safety of the shade our parents stayed, watching us cavort, dive, swim, and when they called to us we went to them reluctantly, not just because we were setting aside the sea and sun, but because we were setting aside our identities as Australian children and joining the lily-white Pommies in the shade.

Our annual summer holidays were sea gifts too and we looked forward to them fervidly all year. My parents saved for these trips from my father's tight salary, and they rented unassuming cottages at Tuggerah Lakes or Toowoon Bay on the Central Coast and Wombarra or Scarborough on the coast just south of Sydney. The irony of the name 'Scarborough' wasn't lost on them. It was always a trigger for another of those 'when we went to …' conversations; the new place the imposter, the old one the true place with its castle and promenade and penny-shoving amusement arcades. In the real Scarborough they played arcade games and ate fish and chips on the pier. They took home Scarborough rock as a souvenir. What did we take back from Sydney's Scarborough? Something to write home about, a place of comparison? They were already drafting their letters to England, I suspect, as we got off the train at Australia's Scarborough and followed Lawrence Hargrave Drive down the hill from the station, the sea on our left already tantalising, the railway line and the escarpment at our right. Down the road with our suitcases and shopping bags we trotted, hearing the call of lorikeets, the crash of the waves and the rumble of a Coalcliff coal train making its way down to the Port Kembla steel works. Once we'd collected the key and turned it in the beach house's door, the first thing my mother always did was to make a pot of tea.

We usually went to these beach houses just after Christmas, which added further excitement to the long, hot summer holidays and more opportunities for photos to send home to chilly England. The houses were former miners' cottages or shacks for the most part – but we lived on the beach anyway, coming home only at dusk and tumbling into bed after a makeshift tea, to be tossed to sleep by the waves that lingered in our bodies long after we had left the sea.

I long for those beaches sometimes, especially when I'm ensnared in a dark and wet Liverpool January. The heat of sun on skin, an elastic week when each day stretched from the wake-up call of a whip bird at dawn to the sunset beyond the Illawarra escarpment, the sea retaining the last light in pink and yellow folds long after the escarpment had been darkened by the relinquished sun. The smell of the coconut oil that asserted itself over the ozone, the rock pools we probed, the tormented cunjevoi, the starfish, the plunge into the still water of a sea pool built as work relief in the Great Depression, running, always running, across soft white sand. Wild places with neat holiday houses nibbling at the edges of bush and water. My parents compared them to Bridlington, Blackpool, and that other Scarborough. No fun piers, no helter-skelter, no penny shove, no bingo, no black pudding and chips, just a corner store on Lawrence Hargrave Drive where my holiday friends and I bought teen magazines full of English pop bands and a liquorice strip so long it lasted the length of the walk from shop to beach. Those coal miners' shacks have been replaced with multi-million dollar houses now, their glass balconies maximizing the sea views. The landscape stays wild around them though, just as our memories do. There's no containing the ocean or the brutal cliffs of the escarpment that rise towards the western sky – a whisper of waterfalls, of gum trees speckled with sulphur-crested cockatoos that shriek to one another as the sun makes a sun dial of the escarpment's stone.

By the 1960s we were firmly established in our house in Bankstown. My parents might still talk with strong Yorkshire accents, with *thee* and *thine* and *ours* and *sups* and *owts*, but their English-born children had lost most of the cultural markers they'd carried with them from Yorkshire and their Australian-born kids were stridently of place. We'd all grown beachy and brown and independent, as witnessed in colour snaps of holidays where we lined up on a kayak at Long Jetty or showed off on the beach in Thirroul. We were still trotted out to be photographed with tubs of tomatoes and grapes from the garden, but now, dressed in shorts and tee-shirts, we squinted inelegantly into the burning sun from under toweling hats, or sucked on chocolate paddle pops or icy poles. And so we took our parents' hands and led them into a different kind of home, somewhere hybrid, somewhere that was neither here nor there. We might still patiently sit through the BBC World Service's football scores or feign an enthusiasm for the Investiture of Prince Charles, but our interest in the old country had waned like a sneakily-retreating tide. We had our own narratives now and England was too far away to be part of them. My friends were undergoing the same transformations. They might be dragged off to Lithuanian dancing classes or Spanish language courses or church socials, but they too were mounting their resistance to all the cultural markers that tied them too closely to their parents' history.

I never asked my parents if this cultural disloyalty caused them any sadness. I wish I had now. How did you feel when your children stopped caring about your past and became robustly Aussie? Did you feel you were losing something of yourself? My parents weren't the type of people to ever talk about their emotions. Their mix of Yorkshire laconism, the seemingly brusque and sullen qualities of Yorkshire-speak combined with an odd kind of suspicion that they might be out of place wherever they went, meant there was no point in trying to pick away at the past with them. Had they responded, I suspect they would have used one of my maternal grandfather's favourite truisms, 'you make your bed and you lie in it' or 'what's done is done.' That would cap off whatever well of feeling might lie below all the hard work and saving and house building and adjusting and assimilating they'd had to do. They might have spoken English and come from Australia's dominant Anglo culture, but they always seemed apologetic about their place in the world. Losing past references generationally must have exacerbated that trait.

My parents seemed radically different from the other English parents I knew. I sometimes found myself watching them as one might watch a unique new animal in a zoo. What were they doing that took them into the zone of difference? Was it the application of Yorkshire meal times, the football, the clothes, the accents? It took me until adulthood to put my finger on it. They were fearful of causing offense and found the ease of Australia's culture less familiar than they'd expected. Not for them the impromptu lunches and barbeques, the car trips to beaches or the Blue Mountains that my uncle and aunt frequently took. For my parents everything needed to be pre-planned and that included the anxiety associated with the event. They had never mixed with people from diverse backgrounds before leaving England so the Yugoslavians, Italian, Greek, Ukrainian, Poles and Maltese with whom I went to school and with whom my father worked just flummoxed them even further. What better raft to cling to than their known English routines?

Both parents were a wonderful source of stories though, and I know these partly led me to becoming a writer. I could listen for hours to their stories about England. The things they did as children, the games, picnics and bluebells. The photos, the magazines, the parcels. These were the props to their little narrative dramas. We held those stories close as one might a sacred relic, and weighed them against our Australian experiences. 'Why do you talk about England so much?' an Australian school friend once asked me. It felt like an insult. I didn't shoot back something about my parents or their influence. I was no doubt reading a book at the time by Enid Blyton or Noel Streatfield and I might have blamed it on that. How else could a child articulate the inculcation of ideas from the lost lives of a parent?

I was never bullied at school, as students from non-English-speaking backgrounds were, because my family were British. It was more a case of mediating a certain eccentricity, like the ways in which my parents lived and spoke. My friends must have experienced racism, but I don't remember ever talking to them about it. I suspect it was largely directed at their parents who were chastised for not speaking English or for taking 'smelly' lunches to work. The late Australian civil servant and social reformer, Peter Wilenski, recalled sitting with his mother on a Sydney railway station and witnessing her being verbally abused because she spoke to him in a language other than English. He remembered the sense of embarrassment, the cruelty of it and a protectiveness, too, for his distressed mother.

My brother-in-law, whose parents are Austrian migrants, certainly experienced teachers who were unkind and unsupportive about his language skills. Even in the 1980s, three decades after that first post-war flush of migration, new migrants experienced similar difficulties in Australian classrooms. As the former Vietnamese refugee, Loan, writes in her essay collection *New Humans of Australia*:

Things were hard for me. I remember getting into trouble when I started kindergarten because I didn't know how to tell the teacher that I needed to go to the toilet and as a result I wet my pants. Instead of helping me, she punished me by making me stand in the corner while the kids laughed and pointed at me. It was horrible ... School was also difficult because I didn't fit in. I still couldn't speak the language well, I wore a handmade school uniform sewed by my mum, and instead of sandwiches like the other kids, I had things like fried rice. As a result, the kids would pick on me and call me things like 'Ching-chong' ... Mum wasn't very sympathetic, as she believed school was for study not for play. When she was young, she had begged her parents to send her to school, but because they were poor and she was a girl, it hadn't been a priority. So she just said to me, 'If they don't want to play with you, don't play with them!'

Given the multi-cultural nature of Australia after the War, reforms took a long time to reach Australian social policy. The federal and state governments of the 1950s and 1960s expected migrants to quickly assimilate, and this expectation was often reflected on or mocked in works like Pino Bossi's novel *Australia Carne* (1988) or the 1966 film *They're a Weird Mob*, based on John O'Grady's book written under the pen name, Nino Culotta. The film was directed by the British filmmakers Michael Powell and Emeric Pressburger and it poked fun at the cultural misunderstandings between

Australians and Italian migrants. The reality was less amusing, especially when the young English-speaking children in a migrant family were required to translate the often-intimate details of a parent's illness or complete a government form for them, or to witness, as had Peter Wilenski, his mother's harassment and humiliation.

With the Whitlam government's reforms came change and a greater understanding of the riches multiculturalism brings to a nation. However, racism still permeated Australian society, as its treatment of its indigenous peoples shows. 'Outsiders' were still viewed with suspicion and hierarchies of migration began to play out, as seen in the mid-1970s when Vietnamese refugees fleeing the fall of Saigon were first allowed into Australia. At the time, racist anti-Vietnamese graffiti began appearing in Greek in Marrickville, the 'old' migrants resenting the new ones. Today, as migrants from Syria and Yemen are left to rot in offshore detention centres, one can only wonder what happened to tolerance in our migrant nation, and why our narratives against recent refugees and migrants have become so cruel.

My childhood memories of my multicultural school seemed removed from much of this. I remember being envious of an Italian classmate whose lunch comprised of pieces of chocolate wedged between thick layers of white bread, or the easy hospitality of Lithuanian and Spanish friends whose mothers cooked food that was exotically tasty. My Aunt Margaret lived next door to Italians who found us children extremely entertaining. Mrs Messetti always seemed to be on hand, watching us over the fence as her husband and son toiled in their tomato garden, or calling to us to come and taste some newly-baked crostoli or cannoli. We once deliberately made one of my cousins weep because we knew she'd be petted by the warm-hearted woman. Our ploy worked. My cousin came back from the concerned Mrs Mesetti's kitchen with a bag of ripe peaches to share.

My school's multicultural students must have been confused by the lessons they were taught. Our maps of the world showed the British Empire in pink and we learned about English Kings and Queens, English wars and heroes. Empire Day was a celebration of all things British and was eagerly anticipated because it was a half-day holiday after which evening bonfires were lit. All the children took party food to school and we consumed it after an Empire Day parade for which we dressed up as representatives of Britain's far-reaching empire. Blackface was used, as were the 'coolie' clothes of colonial Hong Kong. We paraded, the bulk of the class not from British backgrounds at all but from Eastern and Southern Europe, and we sang the national anthem which at that stage was still 'God Save the Queen'. We repeated the pledge that opened every school assembly. 'I honour my God. I serve my Queen. I salute the flag.' Thankfully, this jingoistic Britishness has disappeared and Australian school children now celebrate their indigenous or multicultural backgrounds in school celebrations that invite a diversity of projects, presentations and food from all the countries of the world. These reforms were largely due to the Whitlam government's policies and they offered new ways of rewriting our Australian narrative, one which recognised our indigenous history and the country's multiculturalism.

My parents eventually seemed to adapt with the changing times. They may have joined the throngs who lined Sydney's streets to wave the Union Jack when the Queen or other members of the royal family visited Sydney, but they didn't seem to harbour any resentment about the way Australia's social narrative became more inclusive. In Australia, my father always worked in multicultural workplaces, so I suppose he learned from colleagues. My mother's life was more circumscribed as she remained a 'homemaker' all her life. As their children married, they watched multiculturalism enter the family stories. We are now a blended multicultural family with, to date, English, Italian, Maltese, Austrian, Indian, Lebanese and Irish members; as such, we represent the Australian story of migration and resettlement. I'm sure my parents didn't envisage that when they left Yorkshire.

As I write, I realise just how much of my family's migrant story is from a child's view and perspective – a mediation between parental and sibling stories about what they had gone through and what I drew from my own experiences. To this day, we are all great storytellers, and we argue or debate interpretations and memories. We compare our experiences of the same events – each one lived in numerous different ways. I see this as the filter of my family's Yorkshire history, their prior claim on a former place. Their memories are those of the hypersensitive migrant, observing, absorbing, storing memories that will slowly erode their earlier lives in England. These intergenerational exchanges did not detract in any way from our mind maps, our fictions or exaggerations. We understood the value of these diverse interpretations in our own ways, be they a child's view or an adult's. By valuing all, we add texture and layering, insights and sympathy, a useful technique as Andrea Cleland writes:

To understand how storytelling shapes intergenerational family memories about migration, oral history is a particularly useful technique as it recognises the complex interconnections between migration and the formation of ethnic identities. Memories can provide unique insights into the processes that shape migrant belonging over time, including into diasporic family life from the perspectives of men, women and children. This space of social networks between people is crucial to the experience of migration, although often there is little written about those relations. Despite some limitations, such as memory loss and ethical responsibilities, personal accounts are often the only way to understand migrant experiences.

And so our stories ran on and on like a spool of thread.

As soon as my parents arrived in Bankstown they joined the local Scottish Presbyterian church; for social reasons, I can only presume. They were never particularly religious, but they sent their kids off to Sunday school where we met other English and Scottish children. The church filled a cultural gap, with its fetes and Sunday school anniversaries at which books were presented for attendance and religious instruction. We sang hymns – 'Jesus wants me for a sunbeam', 'The wise man built his house upon the rock' and 'Jesus bids us shine'. We learned about religious figures like Moses or Ruth from workbooks which we illustrated and coloured-in with gusto. Neither of my parents drank alcohol, so a church which expected teetotalism was no great hardship for them. My sister and I attended Sunday school until we graduated to the Fellowship group in our teens, a social rather than religious experience with dances and parentally-supervised barbeques. I enjoyed reading the Bible. I liked the stories and they linger with me still. Even the fate of Ruth was not lost on me, and I would often watch my mother as she read her letters from home and think of homesick Ruth amidst the alien corn.

My parents didn't go to church often but when they did it offered them continuity in their social community. They contributed to the church fetes and helped maintain the church hall and gardens. In Hammerton and Thomson's study of British migrants, a number of the migrants they spoke to referred to their instinctive gravitation towards elderly English friends. My mother was certainly drawn to older women in the church and in her case, I realize now, these older women acted as mother substitutes for the mother she'd left in Yorkshire; a common transference, I imagine, amongst migrant women who missed a close relationship with their mothers, aunts or sisters. All her life my mother maintained those church friendships, even when her real mother had come to live with us.

One of the year's most anticipated social activities was the church's annual picnic day, which I suspect my mother enjoyed because it took her back to the miners' picnic days of her youth. Picnic days always seemed to be sunny. The double-decker buses that transported us to picnic grounds on the shores of Botany Bay waited outside the church hall. On the given Saturday we walked the few blocks along Lancelot Street. There was no need to pack a picnic because lunch was provided by the church, usually in the form of sandwiches, cream buns and the sugary orange cordial which was a ubiquitous presence in my childhood. A towel and swimming costume were all that was needed. Kids piled upstairs on the bus. The parents stayed below. The Sunday school ladies had organized the picnic; the busy-body Mrs Smith and the self-righteous Mrs Jones. I once saw them having a verbal 'stoush', prim in their flowered church hats and rayon Sunday dresses. They argued about who was to do what at the next church fete and who should mind their own business about the cake stall and what not. We sang all the way from Bankstown to Dolls Point or Ramsgate, both beaches on Botany Bay. Iron-railed fences surrounding the sea pool kept sharks and stingrays from the swimming area. We ran ourselves ragged, picnicked, competed in egg and spoon races, and were far quieter on the return trip. At the end of the next day's service we said a prayer of thanks for another successful picnic day.

And so these memories spool and unspool, in what Patricia Hampl has argued is the talent for memory to render detail, to pay homage to the senses, to introduce us to the 'particles of life', the richness and idiosyncrasy of our existence. The function of memory, Hampl believes, is also personal and surprisingly political. Reflecting on the past seems to be so important to us because it anchors our identities in some temporal way, defining us, allowing us to chart our progress through life as a series of remembered events, like monuments scratched into the parchment of an old map.

My school friends who were Roman Catholic went to the Catholic Church in Bankstown, but I don't recall any religious discussion about our respective Sundays. If there was any talk of sectarian difference, it was not in front of us children. We were more attuned to the things we could do away from the parental gaze, those post-church activities that often involved roaming the deserted Sunday afternoon streets with friends or poking around the bush of Black Charlie's Hill, the family dog straining on its leash while we chattered about school or our dreams. This freedom seemed ours from a very young age, demonstrating a parental trust in our new suburb with its wide streets punctuated with remnants of bush. It meant we could head out after our Sunday lunch and not return until dusk, when Dad would be in the garden tilling his vegetable patch and mother was in the kitchen sewing at the kitchen table and listening to the radio. No questions were asked about what we'd been up to.

Would we have experienced this freedom if we had stayed in England? There certainly would have been lots of relatives to visit, cousins to play with, though not our school's ragtag mix of migrant kids from all over the globe. Family – we all missed it. Monkton pit had its own social structures and Royston had pubs, clubs and shops in closer proximity than the less-densely-populated Bankstown with its quarter-acre blocks and picket fences. We dressed up whenever we went on family outings, usually to the beach or annual events like the Royal Agricultural Show at Easter, or a steam train exhibition at Central Station of which I still maintain memories of the huff and puff of steam and gleaming brass train parts. I see today in Sydney's Vietnamese, African and Middle Eastern migrant families the same desire to dress their children in their best clothes for jaunts such as these. It was no different for us and there was no arguing against the neat frocks and net petticoats we'd worn to church. On the Manly ferry, my sister and I looked enviously at children lucky enough to be dressed more appropriately in casual shorts and shifts, while we sat uncomfortably in our stiff and formal clothes.

Was my parents' insistence on such formal clothing a migrant's need to ensure their children maintained the standards of the old cultural regime? A fear of not appearing to take their new migrant responsibilities seriously? However much we protested we had no choice but to do as we were told. It was only when I turned fifteen that I felt able to scandalize my parents by wearing shorts on a shopping trip into Sydney.

Summer holidays. Christmas over. We had been for our annual stay in Wombarra. A residual tan still tinted our arms and shoulders. Our Aunt was taking us into Bankstown to see a film and before the film we would have lunch in the cafeteria of one of Bankstown's department stores. My cousins and I had already decided what we'd eat – a Big Ben pie, mashed potatoes and peas – and after that we'd drink a lime ice-cream soda the colour of a deep-green emerald ring. The department store was the height of shopping sophistication before the Compass Centre, before Bankstown Square or Roselands. In it you could buy clothes and crockery, perfume and makeup. I haunted its aisles after my Saturday visit to the library, spending pocket money on a silver poodle brooch or a raspberry flavoured lipstick. It was my aunt and her friend, Mrs Foster, who introduced me to this suburban sophistication; a first taste of a brandy snap from a cake shop on South Terrace, lunch at a cafeteria, and shop-bought rather than handmade clothes. My aunt understood the Australian need for informality. I would often catch her looking me over sympathetically whenever I was inappropriately dressed to the nines, even for a casual lunch and a film, while her daughters were in summer shifts or shorts. I suspect there were times when she tried to mediate between cultural differences like these – between my parents' belief in dressing up to go out and the Australian practice of dressing down.

By the time my parents had been in Australia for over a decade, things began to change. We kids may have been caught between cultures, but we had learned how to negotiate. We played the good children of Yorkshire at home while forging an Australianness when away from it, and after a few years of duality we realized time had shaped us into something no longer malleable. Those beach holidays and Sunday school picnics, the Easter show, Paddy's market, the picnics and barbeques and school excursions had forged our identities into a toughness that could resist further Anglicisation. Like some crude, hybrid thing we had reshaped ourselves into something startlingly Australian. The outer shell of England had cracked, tentatively at first, then emphatically, as our Australianness emerged. I saw it in myself in those adolescent photos with friends. A day trip to the Roselands shopping centre, a day at Manly beach in our new pink-and-white-checked bikinis, our bucket bags stuffed with beach towels and coconut oil. Surnames meant nothing and we bantered about them, both the English ones like Cole and Prior and Smith and Jenkins, or German, Dutch, Lithuanian, Czech and Spanish names. They were just a lick of parentage. We no longer cared to know about where they'd come from. We were tanned, sporty, free – Aussie girls on an Aussie beach.

Looking back down the long tunnel of those teenage years, I can only see our transformation as a form of necessary rebellion. Our parents were flummoxed at first, then challenged by what they were seeing. They'd lost us. We moved to different rhythms, in different circles, not just our social and friendship circles but the gyring, circling dance of the newly-released – the intoxicated spinning of a new cultural identity.

Whenever I look at David Hockney's swimming pool paintings, a Yorkshireman in love with California, I can't help but see the bright blue rectangle of an Australian backyard swimming pool. Its water ripples and fizzes in the breeze. Insects skim over a surface on which inflated li-los drift. Cicadas whirr mechanically from the gum trees. The scent of a barbeque wafts across the lawn. Sausages, lamb chops, T-bone steaks. Onion rings. We sit around a wooden table, its surface splintered and cracked by the relentless sun. The kids have white noses – zinc cream to protect them from sunburn. They prance about in Speedos and towelling hats. They drink orange cordial and play French cricket.

We would spend hot Sunday afternoons like this at the houses of family and friends – though not in those early years, when life remained financially constrained and adolescence bared its resentments and accusations. Life back then was still lived as though in Yorkshire and I was slowly getting fed up with our family. As far as I was concerned, my parents had spent long enough being British. It had become embarrassing to be Pommies in such an Australian space. How long could the accents, the referential memories keep their hold? Surely not more than two decades?

As I grew older, my adulthood brought the freedom to be myself; I moved away from home into the inner city and cut my ties with suburbia. An artistic circle, a terrace house, pubs, galleries, concerts and university provided an Australian context and a specifically Australian way to live. The gap between my parents and I grew, and this was exemplified as I sat around a family pool or a picnic table, a member of a new Australian generation of young adults; so Aussie, so organic to place, that the old Yorkshire habits of my parents seemed sad, lost, anachronistic. This feeling of optimistic Australian-ness was strengthened by the Labour government. Under Whitlam, British migration was no longer awarded a special status and the British, like my parents, needed to apply for Australian citizenship. Multiculturalism meant being British became part of a wider cultural identity. Wherever you'd migrated from had equal cultural status, and our national diversity was recognized and celebrated. Money was allocated for home-grown films and television that captured this diversity, launching initiatives from the Australian Film Commission to the ABC's commitment to local productions rather than imported offerings from the BBC. The Special Broadcasting Service had been established and it showed films and TV programs from all over the world in their original language. As the Australian children of migrants, my friends and I moved fluidly between our identities. Primarily we defined ourselves in keeping with the country's new pride in its diversity. It was OK to be Greek-Australians, Anglo-Australians, Italo-, Lebanese-, Croatian- or Spanish-Australians, though this might shift again whenever racism called for us to merge or reassert our Australianness. As the Vietnam War ended the country welcomed Indo-Chinese refugees.

For many migrants this transition from British to Australian occurred slowly, shaping, shifting, retreating, advancing. Hammerton and Thompson write:

> Like all migrant identities these were unstable and shifting ... These rich and complex identities, perhaps, are the point at which British migrants share most, with migrants from other backgrounds. The lifelong effects of migration.

The instability underpinning identity affected my generation too. Cultural developments in the home country, such as the Beatles generation in the UK, Carnaby Street and Swinging England made my friends and me regretful that we weren't in the UK experiencing the youth revolution there. We created a proxy experience in our own patch of western Sydney, devouring music and English magazines, adopting hairstyles and clothes meticulously copied from films and magazine articles. It was much later that Italian, Greek or Spanish friends seemed to get access to this kind of proxy, or so it seemed at the time. They were uncool, relegated to their own migrant communities, until their stories were given full vent in parody and film such as the 1987 stage comedy *Wogs Out of Work*, written by Nick Giannopoulos, Simon Palomares and Maria Portesi. *Wogs Out of Work* spawned the television show *Acropolis Now*, a radical program for television at that time. Writing in *Neo Kosmos*, the commentator Fotis Kapetopoulos commented about the show:

> The characters who found life in the sitcom *Acropolis Now* resonated with second-generation Greek, Italian and children of immigrants. For the first time we all saw comedy about us, about our lives that was created by our peers. We recognised the archetypes. It was not Mark Mitchell's hairy, greasy, 'wog', Con the Fruiterer. They were cool in the stonewash jeans and mullet haircuts of the 80s. We heard ourselves, our malapropisms, and saw our (mis) behaviours. We recognised the characterisations of our parents, working in factories, cafes and milk bars. We laughed at our crassness until it ached and forgot our deep self-loathing and faux aspirations. We laughed at the racism that we, including our parents endured. But we laughed from a position of power for the first time. We gave back as well making fun of the button-up and puritan Aussies, who the characters casually called, 'skips'.

Bankstown remains one of Sydney's most ethnically-diverse suburbs, as does the wider region of western Sydney. The suburbs in which my friends and I once roamed are now the homes of narratives about different experiences of migration. In a *Guardian* article 'I didn't want to be a "Lebo" growing up in Australia, but I came to love who I am,' writer Mostafa Rachwani talks about living in Western Sydney as a blend of Lebanese and Australian. Rachwani grew up knowing Lebanon through the rose-tinted glasses of his parents while developing a hybrid local identity, 'Lebo', 'with its own fashion sense, steeped in sports brands, its own complex palette, politics and rough boundaries, over time developing its own sense of self.' Visiting Lebanon for the first time Rachwani found:

> an incredible, complex country, weighed down by its history and politics, bouncing with energy and creativity. Somehow bursting with hope and utterly hopeless at the same time. But certainly not 'my' country. I couldn't imagine their experiences, couldn't connect with what it meant to be Lebanese, not by fault but by design. Simply put, I'd never lived there. The realisation came in waves. I stood out like a sore thumb in a place I'd hoped to just melt away in.

He came to the realisation that eventually overtakes many children of migrants, the products of Australia who straddle two cultures and must cope with all the angst that duality can bring. 'To some degree,' he writes, 'my angst was a product of Australia itself. I did not see myself or my identity in the TV shows I watched, only in the news. Inherently, I hated being Lebo because of the reputation it carried. But it wasn't until I realised that I missed the particular kind of charcoal chicken you can only get in Granville that I came to understand I was denying who I was. I was searching for something I already had. A sense of self, a sense of belonging and understanding. I love my community, warts and all.'

Hybridity seems the word for Australia's waves and waves of migration, in which families such as mine played their own small part. All those migrants since 1788, stealing, appropriating, digging in; the Australian landscape making its own voice heard through floods and fires and droughts. Our summer days at Scarborough often ended with a downpour and thunder above a leaden sea, the sand wind-tumbled. We travelled back to Bankstown through a national park that might be ravaged by bushfires a few weeks after we had returned to school, in new uniforms that smelled of poplin and the department store in which they'd been bought, in new school shoes pinching with the merciless cruelty of hard new leather on sea-softened skin, our books covered in brown paper and a picture cut from a magazine and into which we drafted the inevitable first essay of the term – 'What I did on my summer holidays'.

I haven't been back to Market Street for years but if I go I know I'll find my child-self. She swings on the front gate as she waits for Mr Tweedale to arrive in his Morris Minor. Then the family will cram into the car and Mr Tweedale will drive us to Sunday lunch in Merrylands. Over lunch the adults will reminisce about the north of England. Leaning on the gate and looking right, the child can see the house of her aunt on the opposite side of the road. There will be lunches at her aunt's house too, supplemented by tomatoes from the garden and by the family credo, 'never go anywhere without contributing something to the meal.' From my aunt's house to the garage, then to the fibro house, our family has been slowly digging in to Bankstown. We will go in our own directions in the years to come, to other suburbs, other cities, different countries. None of us will predict these geographical and cultural shifts as we pose for another family photo under the jacaranda, children diminished by being of two places, our identities thinned and spread and stretched to encompass two cultures.

Bankstown of the tree-lined streets, the corner shop, the

Billycarts, the church fetes, the ballet classes, the Sunday school picnics. The cat's piss scent of privet as we waited for the school bus, the frozen cordial bottles, the Vegemite sandwiches in school lunchboxes, those lunches eaten on benches in the shade in a playground crozzled by century high temperatures. Upside down, we experienced the seasons in counter order. Hot Christmases, Easters dissolving into the crisp authority of autumn. Our family too far away to see at weddings, Christenings, funerals – those rituals imprinted on paper, letters, cards, photos, their griefs, joys and optimisms papery too.

Our dreams included good health and education, an outdoor lifestyle, an ongoing interest in sport. It would take the Whitlam government to enshrine these dreams in social policy. Medibank, free tertiary education, arts funding for an Australian film industry, ballet, opera, literature; indigenous affairs and fault-free divorce and anti-discrimination laws. These further shaped and defined who we were, and added a layer through multiculturalism. In Australia, post-1972, the new generation of Australians could be proud about their Australianness as well as their cultural backgrounds. This era went a long way towards reducing social conservatism in Australia such as that sent up by Barry Humphries through his character, Dame Edna Everage, who resided in Melbourne's stuffy, middle-class suburb, Moonee Ponds. The English fashion model, Jean Shrimpton, had experienced this parochialism at the races in Melbourne when she failed to wear gloves or stockings to the Melbourne Cup, much to the chagrin of Melbourne's society matrons who also complained that Shrimpton's skirt was too short. Books were banned too, so novels like James Joyce's *Ulysses* or Philip Roth's *Portnoy's Complaint* were sold in brown paper bags from under bookshop counters. A new generation of Australians politicised by the Vietnam War and later by Whitlam's sacking by the Governor General in 1975 were ready for and expected change. Music was significant in this shift. From Elvis Presley and the British bands of the 1960s to the Beach Boys, Joni Mitchell, Dylan, Baez and the rock musical, *Hair*, our adolescent freedoms, our protests and access to social reforms were accompanied by a musical soundtrack that soon included Australian bands.

Migration, it seems, is a double-edged sword, a Janus mask, a backhanded compliment. You leave, you gain. You remember, you forget. You create new memories as you pass from one state to another, worlds supplanting worlds. In the push and pull of my life, I have sometimes wished that my parents had stayed where they were; for their sakes, not ours. If they had stayed where they were they'd have been of their own place. They'd have endured Margaret Thatcher's destruction of the North, watched mining communities crushed, been poorer, more culturally constrained, but they'd not have carried that migrant reticence that dogged them all their lives if they'd been back in Yorkshire, surely – that apologetic self-consciousness that always made them seem they were in the wrong place, at the wrong time. Over this demeanour hovered a question: would their lives have been better had they stayed?

None of this explains the real pull of migration, the better, safer, richer, happier life for the kids that drove my parents onto the *Empire Brent*. It drew them to Australia like fish on a line. They bravely travelled and it paid off. They both died in the knowledge that their children and grandchildren were more prosperous, educated and confident than they otherwise would have been. There is something humbling in the way they sacrificed their own community to build a new one 12,000 miles away. John Berger wrote of the 20th century in his essay 'Ev'ry Time We Say Goodbye':

> Ours is the century of enforced travel, of disappearances. The century of people helplessly seeing others, who were close to them, disappear over the horizon.

We forged a new identity, avoiding, we hoped, all that was negative about nationalism. John Douglas Pringle called the search for an Australian identity 'that aching tooth.' Others were equally ambivalent about it. The author David Malouf believed Australia was 'endlessly fussing and fretting over identity' while the poet Les Murray described Australian identity as an obsession which 'cripples the spiritual energies.' Identity played a key role in the way my family defined itself. Becoming Australian was also in its own, odd way, a testament to my parents staying British.

CHAPTER FIVE
Return

When I was a teenager my friends and I went through a phase of learning all the songs that the British singer Dusty Springfield had made famous. Songs by Jaques Brel or Charles Aznavour, or Springfield's take on Motown, were belted out in our bedrooms when parents were away. A particular favourite was Springfield's version of Carole King's 'Going Back.' That song seemed to point to a path that loomed some distance ahead of us, yet already we understood its pathos and regrets. Perhaps we had imbibed them as we grew up, those parental anxieties cloaked in wanting the best for their kids. We knew one thing for certain though; as soon as we were old enough we were going to travel back to the places our parents had talked about, to the places our parents had known so well in their youth.

Time passed quickly in the new land; summers long and draped with humidity, rainy winters, springs in which the garden seemed to become one giant, buzzing bee. Before my family knew it, we were settled, though England still maintained its net of influence over my parents in all kinds of ways. *The Dalesman* arrived regularly and both parents still spoke in an idiom enlivened by their Barnsley accents. They continued to eat tea at 5pm and partake of a long supper at 8pm. This substantial meal of sandwiches, biscuits, sweets and pots of tea was part of an old timetable that had its roots in the working-class meals of Royston's miners just off a shift or requiring food to sustain them from an exhausted sleep to a predawn rising. Australian television was complicit in this referential life. All the channels broadcast

British programs and we watched them avidly. Kitchen sink dramas like *Coronation Street*, historical adaptations and police procedurals were viewed with a kind of reverse *déjà vu*, and their underpinning reflection was that we could have been those people and lived in those places.

Was this done with deep personal regret? By the time the family had been twenty years in Sydney, probably not, but my siblings and I certainly emulated English fashion, read English teen magazines, followed English pop groups and mimed singers like Dusty Springfield. We still followed English football teams too – my father remaining loyal to Leeds United until his death. We ate English food whenever possible. When our grandmother came to live with us, she felt like an unwelcome intrusion into all this Englishness. The *faux* Britain we had created from a distance was fine, but to have a living example of it in our midst was not reassuring. If Gran was a representative of all those relatives we'd missed out on, perhaps it was good to have put 12,000 miles between us.

All this changed as we grew up and left home. My older sister went back to England first, to the country she'd left as a three-year old. My brother worked in western NSW and there met the woman he would marry. Eventually, I moved away too. The Vietnam War and Gough Whitlam's Labour government had politicised me and my friends, and our participation in anti-war protests and political activities tethered us in a new way to a new kind of Australia. The Labour government's multiculturalism reminded us of those early years when all our families came in the same boats, migrants with diverse memories of diverse places. Under Whitlam, new ministries began addressing Australian identity through social policies, and indigenous Australians were given a greater voice through government departments which addressed their social inequalities.

I have always believed that each generation needs reforms such as these on which to pin optimism and the hope that a better future awaited. My parents may have missed out on Clement Attlee's reforms in the UK, but my generation had our equivalent in a new Labour government in Australia. Prime Minister Gough Whitlam was my hero. He was someone who took a good look at the country's colonial British identity and gave it a shake, like a dusty old rug in need of a good bashing. In the three short years of his government my parents seemed to let go of what they had been, and what they might have been, and rethought many of the narratives of the past that had sustained them. England may still have been a sentimental lost homeland, but the new one felt more optimistic and so my parents turned towards a different future.

This grasping of reality and a new identity has been described by James Wood as the way 'home swells as a sentiment because it has disappeared as an achievable reality.' England was now just a memory and that was fine by us. It served as a sentimental touchstone, an antipodean narrative about the way we once were. It was fine to accept that we were Australian and that return would be more fraught and dangerous than just staying put.

Soon my parents had lived in Australia for almost as long as they had lived in Yorkshire. Despite this, there still was an unsettling confusion about which place to call home. It was a syndrome described in the old adage – *you can never go home*, though they were certainly planning a visit. Eventually we all returned in our own specific and different ways.

The compulsion to return is embedded in each memory of departure, George Kouvaros wrote in *The Old Greeks*. Return when it came for my family required a slow and reflective transit back. What drove us differed between each of us kids. My sister wanted an adventure and an opportunity to see the country she'd left as a child. She departed Sydney on one of the ocean liners of the *Flotto Lauro* fleet. By the time she returned to Australia a year later, her itch to know England seemed to have been sated; though future trips were made to visit relatives with whom she'd become close on that first return. My brother went on a cruise for his honeymoon on the P&O liner *Canberra*, not to England but on a voyage that seemed to play with that possibility as the *Canberra* dropped in on the west coast of America, Japan and Southeast Asia. His sea voyage also nudged at the edges of his need to return. He would go back to England eventually, many years later, but for short trips and always by plane.

My parents went back together only once, just after my father retired. We had a party for them before they left but there was some apprehension about how they would react to what they found. Thomson and Hammerton note, 'return is never easy and places of the heart rarely stay the same.' The whole family hoped our parents' trip would be a great awakening for them – an opportunity to discover so much about their younger selves and all the people they'd left behind. Unfortunately, my father needed an emergency operation while he was there and, always someone who feared hospitals, he was miserable and made everyone around him miserable too. If I examine that experience now, I wonder just how much his illness debilitated and babyfied him, acting in some Freudian way as a means by which to avoid the questions such a return might throw up. Was it too painful to coolly regard the country he had left behind, or to experience any long-suppressed regrets? Was his illness a way to render himself unable to observe the lost country first-hand, so he viewed it from the restrained and supportive environment of a hospital bed? When he returned to Sydney, my father made it clear to anyone who would listen that the trip had convinced him he'd done the right thing in migrating to Australia. He claimed to have enjoyed his travels, had loved catching up with family, but the social circumstances of the families he'd left hadn't impressed him. He was better off in Sydney. The weather, the garden, the increasing opportunities for and prosperity of his children verified this view. He never went back.

My mother told a different tale of the trip. She had loved being in the UK and I am sure having my hospitalized father out of her hair meant she was free to enjoy her large family in her own ways. They took her on day trips and she was photographed repeatedly, looking happy, eating an ice-cream on an English beach, smiling with sisters and brothers and those nieces and nephews she'd only just met. After my father died she went back a few more times, and from each trip she harvested a narrative from her lost family that sustained her through her final decades.

Soon I was planning my own trip, one that would take me back to my parents' history but would also allow me to set a path of my own through the UK, then Europe and Scandinavia. My return journey would be undertaken by sea. The trip was a long time in planning. As soon as I'd begun work as a civil servant I'd started saving for it, steadfastly economizing so I could book a passage on a ship to England followed by twelve months backpacking around Europe. Today it's called a gap year, as though a great chasm is needed to separate ourselves from the former place – not geographical but personal, a widening space between our youth and maturity, a holiday that makes us wiser to the differences in the world, and the similarities. This would mature us in much the same ways a wayward Prince Hal must set aside all that is youthfully frivolous to become King Henry in Shakespeare's *Henry V*. Travel would broaden us to possibility and allow us to face adult responsibility.

I've already described the ship that took me to England, the *Taras Shevshenko*. What was also important were the ship's other passengers, who seemed divided into two groups: young Aussie travellers with an extended holiday in their sights, and older English people returning after a long time away, perhaps for a holiday as my parents had done or, now elderly, to retire in their place of birth. I remember watching Michael Apted's film, *The Triple Echo*, in the *Taras Shevshenko's* cinema. The film starred Glenda Jackson and included a scene when she opened an oven door to examine a roasting piece of meat, its skin dark red and spitting and glistening with lard. A collective moan of delight rose from the elderly members of the audience. It may have been a response to the rather dire quality of the Russian ship's food, but I suspect it was far more visceral than that. Here again was the cry I'd heard my mother make after fourteen years of exile in Sydney, when she saw her mother at the rails of the *Himalaya* as the ship nosed her way into her berth at Circular Quay. That beef was about as British as you could get, cooking as it was in an old Aga in an historical English cottage in the autumnal English countryside. Perhaps the audience's response was as primal as that made by Ulysses on his return sighting of Ithaca or the Venetians when they heard again the campanile from the bell tower of St Marks. I looked around the dark cinema at old faces illuminated by the promise of the past, those memories of Sunday roasts in meaner kitchens than Glenda Jackson's filmic one, and roasting joints that would soon be available to them if their pensions stretched that far.

For the young Australians on board, the horizon held different promises – some reliving of their parents' pasts certainly, but also new ways in which to secure a hold on their birthright. We would wander into the homes of relatives we had met only on paper; robust, greedy for experience, arrogant in our freedom. The children of the antipodes, we scrounged free beds and meals without batting an eyelid, the only price a little smile when told we looked like the brother or sister of their memories, held like a flash photo from decades ago. The recession the UK was experiencing in the 1970s gilded us with the glow of privilege. How could we possibly afford to travel for a whole year? On our savings? I also saw how a returning migrant's dreams might be shattered. The price of lamb and beef – and certainly the kind of joint I'd seen in *The Triple Echo* – had pushed such a luxury beyond the budgets of most people.

I was travelling to snatch at all those images I'd seen in English magazines and on TV. By the time I turned up in England many of my relatives had moved from Yorkshire to Kent, Hampshire or the Isle of Man, but some remained in my parents' old village. I dutifully visited them all. Some were not living as prosperously as their letters had indicated, but they still seemed buoyed by the strength of family. These were the English mob from whom my parents had removed us. The gap, I realised, created by distance, resolve, economics, or education, was insurmountable. Unlike the close relationships with our few relatives in Sydney, we would never regain a family closeness, though through my own and a niece's reverse migration to England and visits to Australia by our English family, we have recently re-contoured something of what was lost.

The *Taras Schevchenko* carried us home, children drawn to a parents' fairy tale. The ship pulsed and rolled and glided over the oceans, displaying what Horatio Clare has described as a spirit felt in 'the deserted spaces of the poop, the low deck at the stern where the water boils up below you thrashed to white fury by the propeller.' The screens on the bridge gazing forward, 'unblinking eyes staring down at the sea roads of the world, at the thousands of nautical miles and storms and calm to come.' And then, as the *Taras Schevchenko* made her way along the Solent, I regarded with curiosity my parents' home country.

In 'Avoiding it: Writing fiction about place without writing about it,' Rhett Davis talks of England as a country known before being known:

I dream about Britain long before I live there. I see rolling green hills, ancient yew trees, hedgerows and lanes and stone fences and tea-stained brooks, villages and cobblestones and collapsed follies, crumbling castles overlooking valleys. To me it is mystical, a series of visions passed down through hazy genetic memory. Australia, the strange dry, flat country I was born in, had nothing to do with me. But the Britain I naively imagine, that has been passed down to me or I have conjured from my mother's favourite bucolic British television, isn't there. There's a moment, in Wales, next to an abandoned castle, as the sun kisses lush sheep-heavy fields, when I think: yes, maybe, maybe it was here. But the moment passes and the sun sets.

England, the home that never was, not for me, anyway. It was just a chimera, an imagined place made real by being draped with other peoples' memories. My parents had made a good job of embellishment. Here were the corner stores and pubs and commons and woods they'd stitched into our imaginations as we grew up in Sydney. My brother's Hornby train set and its little lead people, its tin stations and signal boxes come alive. The photos in *The Dalesman* and the fashion magazines I had devoured, the bonhomie of village life courtesy of the BBC. Here it all was.

I disembarked in Southampton on an April day still clutching at winter chill. The sun shone as one of my uncles drove me through the New Forest to Bournemouth, where he and my aunt now lived. The New Forest's oaks and forest ponies were soon relegated by suburbs, the mirror-houses so similar in style I asked if they were social housing. This caused some mirth – 'no, people with a bit of money live in those.' I looked again, recalibrating what wealth might mean to dull houses in southern England. If migration is 'defined not by singular moments of departure and arrival, but by a series of gradual transformations, negotiations, and adaptations, understood often only in hindsight,' as Kouvaros maintains, then my disembarkation was all these things in reverse; an old film rewound, a slow-motion replay as the landscape – so familiar in its unfamiliarity – unspooled before me.

Writing about V.S. Naipaul, Ian Baucom reflects on how Naipaul only fleetingly registers London in his text, and when he does acknowledge the city, it is as a site of disappointment. 'I had come to London,' Naipaul says, 'as to a place I knew very well. I found a city that was strange and unknown … The disturbance in me, faced with this strangeness, was very great.' Naipaul's disturbance, Baucom writes, 'is not only a response to what he does not find in London – the city's obliterated addresses and those "British things" to which he had imagined the great city was home – but what he does find there. He discovers not the metropolitan seat of the imaginary England in which he had come to believe, but a city of migrants, a city filled with people such as himself.'

I travelled around England, creating a new map to be placed over the old map my family history had already drawn. Not the tourist maps of castles and stately homes, the heritage-listed villages or the pilgrimages to the homes or graves of literary heroes. This new map confirmed or redrafted the stories we had been fed in Sydney. The family-referenced houses, shops and churches were claimed and gathered like a kind of deeply personal family Monopoly game.

Over the next 12 months I did a lot of things – all firsts. The first ferry to Calais. The first train to Paris and the cheap hotel in St Germain des Pres. Amsterdam, Munich, the Greek Islands. North to Scandinavia, to snow in Flam and Bergen, south to Italy and Venice, Florence, Rome. But it was England that required more of me than the adolescent, peripatetic crawl through the beautiful cities of Europe. In England I had to test myself to see which parts remained of my parents' pasts, and which were truly me.

I took jobs close to another aunt's place near Christchurch in Hampshire. Washed dishes in a *Little Chef*. Made components in a factory, meeting people for whom this was work and not just a tourist's pocket money. I caught a train up to London and stayed in a Shepherd's Bush B&B. Then, after acclimatising to the weather and the oddness of being Australian in Bournemouth, with its beach and rundown seafront, its pleasure gardens and pier, I bought a 49cc Mobylette moped and set out to explore England properly.

I didn't head north straight away. I'm not quite sure why. Perhaps it was my aunt's proximity to the West Country and to the lovely coast of Dorset and Devon. Or was it the ease with which I could first explore Thomas Hardy country? From there I headed down the length of Cornwall, by then in need of the sandy beaches I was missing in Sydney. The north pulled, though, so I slowly travelled up

there on my little scooter, through Oxford, Bath, Glouces-
ter, Chester then through Manchester to Macclesfield and
the Peak District, by-passing Sheffield by heading straight
for Royston.

It is hard to capture that moment, late in the day, my
backside sore from a long day's ride on my moped, of arriv-
ing in the town where my parents had met and married, to
see on the side of a pub a big painted sign, *Barnsley Bitter*.
There was the 12th century church in which my parents
were married, the sign to Monkton Pit and some graffiti supporting Leeds United and the team's captain, Billy
Bremner. I asked directions to my uncle's house and experienced the first shock of recognition that would shake each
new encounter – the slowly-delivered words in the strong
South Yorkshire accent I had grown up with in Sydney. By
the time I left England a year later, torn between going back
to Australia and staying put, I understood more about why
my parents had decided to get away and what they'd have
been had they stayed.

Riding a moped all around the UK is a book within itself.
I had never ridden a motorbike or scooter before but after a few weeks of wobbling education I soon learned the
technique. I welcomed the intimacy with the countryside
through which I was travelling. Dorset had been first, with
its heady fragrance of hay and yellow gorse, the scent of it
honeyed and intoxicating. I had followed the coast to Lyme
Regis, ambled through Dartmoor and Exmoor. I had travelled all the way down to the tip of Cornwall, often pushing
the moped up hills too perpendicular for its engine. Next
came the West Country, the Midlands, Yorkshire, Cumberland, a foray into Scotland then back south through Lincoln,
Norfolk and Cambridgeshire, where the moped packed it

in just outside Ely. There was a lot less traffic on the roads then, so I travelled without the fear that engulfs me these days whenever I enter a British motorway. The country unfolded slowly, languidly, wetly, through weeks and months of crossing it. I hadn't expected the regional diversity of it. Despite those teen magazines and the BBC, I had interiorised a very specific and parental northern identity, yet in some metaphysical way my travels were like traversing the supine body of a mother, an exploration of all the known but unknown body parts that had previously been private, secret even. I didn't know this intense feeling again until I sponged my father's dying body. It was an enigma, all that previously untouched parental flesh. With my father I was discovering and losing it at the same time and the feeling was overwhelming in its melancholy burden.

As I travelled, I hunted, especially in Yorkshire, for those murmured places of family folk stories, the bluebell woods that emerged as I rode towards Leeds, a carpet of blue like lapis lazuli, known but new. The smell of coal and sulphur that rose from Monkton Pit. The freshly fried fish and chip smell of the local chippie. My nose, buried in a bag of sweets just bought from a sweetshop full of bull's eyes and aniseed balls and all the other sweets of parental childhood. In my father's stories I'd seen him as a lad with a lump of coal, slinging it at an old tin bath hanging on the outside wall of a house, then darting away as the owner came roaring out at the clang of coal on tin. 'Duck stone' the game was called. A boyish game to drive adults mad. I was overtaken by the taste of pomfret cakes, of proper Yorkshire puddings, the scent of coal fires in a narrow grate, the rolled tobacco smell of the local pub.

If the children of migrants are endowed with anything that can be specifically identified as a special gift, it must be this pre-lived life in a place they are yet to visit and the surge of recognition that overwhelms them when they enter the reality. The writer Oscar Schwartz speaks of it in his piece about New York, 'On Leaving a City', a place made familiar by his parents' stories:

For the past six weeks, ever since my decision to leave New York was final and the flights booked, a song has been running through my head. 'Alexandra Leaving' by Leonard Cohen. It is extremely melancholy, and I wish I could get it out of my head. One line in particular keeps repeating: "Do not say the moment was imagined. Do not stoop to strategies like this." I haven't listened to the song in years, but I think it came back to me because this line seems to capture this thought about New York I'm trying to convey. In a city that is experienced as an idea and a memory before you've even been there, how can you tell what you alone experienced, and what was given to you by others?

The same applied to all the relatives, those photos made flesh. Smaller, ruddier, thinner or meaner, they were suddenly real. These first meetings often required a sort of mediation between the real and imagined parties, like a coming to terms with one another's language. The former generosity of an auntie's parcels might be met with parsimony, an uncle's chattiness in letters with silence in person. The shock of the Yorkshire bluntness that had never quite left my parents but which they managed to smooth the corners of a little in Sydney, was suddenly, brutally there in the little sadistic jokes an uncle or an aunt liked to play, or a comment about how I looked. 'Ye look like thee father, mournful-like,' was my first greeting from an old aunt. 'If you want to know your shortcomings you won't find more helpful people anywhere,' Bill Bryson wrote of Yorkshire folk in *The Road to Little Dribbling*, and that was certainly the case of my mother's family. There was suspicion too, that I had come to visit them but they could not afford, at that time anyway, to come and visit us.

Going back throws the initial departure into a different perspective. What had my relatives thought when my mother and father decided to migrate? I know they were surprised because one of my father's brothers told me this. He was taken aback when his younger brother announced his decision to the family. Our Jack? The indulged sugar baby? The older brother looked at the younger brother with new eyes. There was steely resolve under the sugar coating, it seemed. Others, such as one of my mother's sisters, thought my parents wouldn't be able to hack all that was needed to re-establish themselves in a new country. They would be back – I can still hear the cattiness and the Yorkshire drawl in her words – they'd return, chastened and settle again into Royston life. There must have been sadness too about the cutting of ties, my mother's sisterly closeness, the brotherly jokes of my father's far older brothers and their teasing directed at a much younger sibling. The decision must have ignited ambition and wanderlust in their families too. Three of my mother's siblings would subsequently migrate to Australia, though only one stayed, and numerous others – siblings, nieces, nephews and their progeny – would eventually come for short holidays.

Is departure a persistent stain, offering only despoilment? A shadow texture, the unsociable counter-hew spread across memories? All those fly-spotted photos we didn't see – the awkward one, an uncle's eyes closed against the sun, an aunt talking so her mouth is a blur of words, the silly fixed smile of a cousin too self-conscious to show a missing tooth or a double chin. These are the family members I know now as I travel between them, not the people in the studio photos, not the specially chosen photos for the antipodes, too much like my father's neatly posed piles of grapes and tomatoes that belied the homesickness he'd sown into the ground that grew them.

A whole year of travel. Courtesy of my Eurail pass, I zigzagged my way across Europe by train, bus and boat. I was intoxicated by the excitement of new places, learning something further of my childhood friends' histories in the process. Amsterdam, Germany, Norway, Greece, Italy – I had Australian friends from all these places. I made friends with people making the same pilgrimages, most of us from former colonies of the UK or from countries that had been war-ravaged when their parents left them. In European cafes or youth hostels we shared stories and tips, and occasionally a photo of a newly-met grandmother or aunt or uncle or cousins. We laughed at encounters at which we'd all come to know what it meant to be different, un-belonging, othered, in a place that had once seemed a birthright.

After a year of movement, I grew homesick for Sydney's beaches and barbeques, for frangipani flowers, for family lunches and birthdays, for the smells and sounds of the Australian bush. All those things I'd taken for granted in Sydney now seemed to offer an imperative: 'Come home.' Sick of cheap bed and breakfasts and their mean landladies, of hotels and my relatives' spare bedrooms, I was craving a little house of my own back in Australia; a sunny house with a garden, and for a space that offered me artistic expression. I would buy a house that was as far removed aesthetically from the garage in Bankstown as from the terrace houses of Royston. I had experienced them both now, had come from one to the other and to a great realisation: that my parents ran from one prison to a similar one, albeit with sunnier weather, more land and better prospects for their children. Those things that trapped them in their Englishness in Sydney – their origins, accents, backgrounds and psychopathologies – no longer applied to me. I understood them, but I was not like them. I could go home and become more rooted in *my* Australia.

I made my return journey slowly by sea, on the Chandris lines' *Australis*, via South Africa, Fremantle, Melbourne and Sydney. The *Australis* stopped in Cherbourg then Tenerife in the Grand Canaries, then she followed the west coast of Africa until she reached Cape Town. From there it was a tedious ten days to Fremantle on a choppy and cold Great Southern Ocean. During that time I reflected on all that I'd seen. I would discover, on my return to Sydney, that my parents had saved every aerogramme and postcard I'd sent them. I have these still and they resonate with each gush of discovery, with youthful freedom and the novelty of independent explorations. Everything was so new to me. What could I make of what I'd seen, I wondered. How would my travels shape the way I could now live? What would I do with my newly-discovered family; not the people I'd met in England but the Australians awaiting me? How would my discoveries shape and recalibrate our family story? I pondered all these questions as the *Australis* made her way up Sydney Harbour; through the sandstone portals of North and South Heads, past Nielsen Park, Rose Bay, past the Garden Island naval base, past Taronga Park Zoo, Pinch Gut, the Opera House, into the overseas terminal of Circular Quay.

I was met on the wharf by family, including two new nieces who had been born while I was away, and an overwhelming sense of home. Not the *faux* home conjured from my parents' English memories, but my lived childhood home of ferries and harbour, of heat and magpies and kookaburras, of sunhats and zinc noses. Passport control, Customs, luggage, then the drive home took me west, back to my parents' fibro house where I stayed until I found a flat near Centennial Park in Sydney's Eastern suburbs.

Much had happened in Australia's political life while I was away. I had kept up with it as best I could on visits to London and Australia House in the Strand, where I caught up on newspapers and letters sent to the *poste restante* there. The Whitlam government was under siege from a relentlessly critical and conservative press. The news bitterly documented the cabinet's social initiatives like the Family Law Act, Medibank, government ownership of the fuel resources in the North West Shelf, fee-free university education, job training and employment schemes, multicultural and Aboriginal affairs. The city of Darwin had been devastated by Cyclone Tracey in late 1974 and the government, and Whitlam in particular, were attacked about the handling of the crisis. Over the next twelve months the Whitlam government battled its critics until, in November 1975, it was dismissed by the Queen's representative, the Governor General, Sir John Kerr.

While travelling around Britain I'd had plenty of time to experience and reflect upon class and what it means to people. As a tourist, and a young Australian one at that, you're travelling in a bubble of freedom and privilege. The jobs I undertook were never as meaningful to me as they were to the local people for whom they meant food and a home. I often found myself chatting with people from all walks of life who were curious about the array of souvenir badges on my backpack. Had I really visited all those countries? As I worked in a factory or café, I met students from British universities, young working-class parents, old coal miners as well as Americans and Swedes and French and Germans on a long summer break from their work and study routines at home. I reflected on what I'd be doing had my parents stayed in England. Would I be a working-class Yorkshire lass with a strong Barnsley accent? Would I have gone to university? Travelled? Would my pocket-money job have sustained my life in a place like Royston?

These questions retreated over the next twelve months when, back at work, I saved the deposit for a cheap terrace house in Sydney's Surry Hills. It wasn't unlike the little English terraces of my relatives, and I'd sometimes see a puzzled look creep over my father's face as he took in its steep staircase and two upstairs bedrooms and the tiny kitchen. I should have joked with him and said, 'see what you did,' but he hadn't done anything at all. I was just one of an army of young people who'd made our rite of passage by backpacking around the world and who were now looking for a place of our own. We wanted a cheap inner-city terrace as far from Sydney's suburbia as we could get. We didn't want the embroidered wall hangings of a past life in Eastern Europe, or the tea and parkin of Yorkshire. What we wanted wasn't from our parents' culture – it was Australian, and it was framed within a narrative of multiculturalism and adventure. We'd learned about other places and we were happy to embrace them once we got home, reliving meals in Italy or Florence in Sydney's Italian restaurants in Leichhardt or the Italian Club in Railway Square, or Baltic meals in Taylor Square and Greek meals in Newtown. We bought cookbooks that took us back to our travels as well, learning more from local chefs like Don Dunstan or Bernard King than from mothers and grandmothers who had grown up in the traditions. My terrace house was transformed with quarry tiles and Danish design, Ikea, pot plants and flokati rugs. And there I stayed until I'd saved enough to travel to England again.

The Vietnam War turned my attention away from Europe and towards Southeast Asia, but unlike teenage friends who saved up for a trip to Bali or Lombok, my travel sights remained firmly set on Britain. I needed to get that first British and European trek out of my system before considering any travel closer to home, so I travelled in Australia for a while before making my second trip to the UK. I visited Tasmania, Victoria and Queensland, usually by train. I enjoyed bush walking so these trips often involved a stay in a place where I could explore the Australian bush, but hitch-hiking holidays were also spent thumbing my way from beach to beach. These trips provided a sense of space that I hadn't expected. I stood on the bluffs of Southern Queensland's Lamington National Park looking towards Murwillumbah, and NSW stretching out in the distance. I could walk for days without seeing another person. In the Outback I was surprised by Chinese restaurants, Greek cafes, Italian pizza joints, by the local Aboriginal people window-shopping wistfully in what passed as shopping strips. It was the reflective times when the sadness caught me – a sense of something my parents had missed in their own places – a darkening road, my hotel still kilometres away. If any vehicle passed me, whoever was driving would raise their forefinger slowly from the wheel, the lazy salute of the Australian outback traveller. Out in the bush the night creatures were mustering. The birds were swarming by the waterholes. Lights had gone on in little towns. And headlights offered their beams to the long, lonely stretch of road.

Perhaps this is why the first thing that struck me on that first visit to England was the crowded nature of it; or so it had felt, until I first encountered the spaces of the Dales or the North Yorkshire Moors and recalibrated my understanding of Britain's spatial mass. If Australia is a vast continent with its population clinging to its coast, then England is surely akin to Dr Who's Tardis; its teeming cities, its terrace houses, its population somehow managing to fit into crowded cities but also endowed with great swathes of moors and crags and hills.

I have been back to England dozens of times since then for holidays, for work, sometimes visiting family and sometimes not. The second of my trips involved a six-month sabbatical from my civil service job. During that trip I extended my previous parameters with long-distance walks along Offa's Dike, the South Downs, the Pennine Way, rediscovering in the process just how far family roots extended beyond the Royston-Barnsley-Sheffield map my parents had trod. Visiting relatives was less of an imperative on that trip, and I felt freer as a result. I had no one to meet, no quest, no probing to do. I had cast off the burden of a mixed identity and could just be an Australian doing what other Australian tourists were doing.

Even back then, I found England's obsession with World War II rather disturbing. Where did it come from? Most of the people who sang wartime songs or eulogised the war weren't even born when the war ended. It was as though a whole generation had been infected with a particularly pernicious form of nostalgia that caused them to become teary-eyed at the mention of Winston Churchill or Vera Lynn. I asked numerous people about this and no one had an answer. I presumed it was a kind of identity politics, an Englishness that must be sustained by regular servings of a life none had lived. Decades later, the British film and television industries remain complicit in this narrative. On a Saturday night, *Dad's Army*, a television comedy set during the war and first broadcast in 1975, is still shown in a prime-time slot. Films like *Darkest Hour* and *Dunkirk* were made in 2019 and 2020 to critical acclaim and box-office success. During the Covid pandemic and Brexit, the jingoistic slogans of Churchill were used to rev up the nation by a Prime Minister who has biographized the wartime leader and who openly claims his style of rhetoric.

I wasn't confronted with this during my first visit when the country, pre-Thatcher, still seemed to pride itself on a wide range of narratives; from the working class and trade union voices of industrial collectivism to the social commentary of films like those of Ken Loach. Perhaps this was because the people who had actually fought or survived the war as adults were still alive, and knew the horrors of it first-hand. I wandered around absorbing all these things – in a pub in Yorkshire or an art house cinema in London, in conversations with a jellied eel stall-holder in Petticoat Lane or a pub landlady in Oxford. The country felt more tolerant then.

I find this tolerance today in Liverpool though, which like most port cities has long been open to people from all cultures and political perspectives. A curiosity about country seems to permeate Liverpool conversations. It doesn't matter where you're from, as long as you like Liverpool. Politics is more tribal, and an insult to one is an insult to all. The *Sun* newspaper has been banned from the city; no-one buys it after its scurrilous attacks on Liverpool football fans at Hillsborough. Liverpool hasn't much time for WWII or Winston Churchill, who threatened to bombard the city if its dockworkers went on strike. The city was also bombed as badly as London by the German Luftwaffe during the

1940 blitz, and it took until the 1970s before much of that damage was repaired. Why be nostalgic for a war and a wartime leader when successive Conservative governments have continued to wage war against your city?

I also noticed a lot more wealth in London on my second visit in the early 1980s. This was the era of the 'hooray Harrys'. Porsches and champagne. Rising house prices. Deindustrialisation and doors closing on public spending and social initiatives. Privatisation. These excesses seemed to quickly become normalised political ideologies. By the 1990s Australia had adopted them too.

England remains a country that sees itself as one of the great democratisers, offering political stability and governance advice to countries around the globe. Brexit and Covid have challenged this image. Any sense of irony seems lost on its leaders. As someone who has grown up in a country which has laws that require its citizens to vote, and an electoral system that has preferential representation, Britain's clinging to 'first past the post' voting is flummoxing. How can a country that prides itself on its democracy not have a fairer and more representative parliament? Why haven't successive governments tackled this iniquity, especially governments like that of Tony Blair with its decade of parliamentary hegemony? A referendum such as the Brexit vote could not have happened in Australia, whose referenda constitutionally require a majority of votes in a majority of states for a referendum to be passed. The Brexit vote, with its narrowest of margins, disregarded the vote to remain in the EU of Scotland, Northern Ireland and Gibraltar. Liverpool voted in favour of remaining in the EU by a margin of 68%.

Now I work in Liverpool, and that old family haunting has resurfaced in a different way. As I've grown older, more professionally connected to travel as research, I find myself looking again for family as though there might be an important text I've missed, as though life is just a prolonged literature review which points you in the direction of all the references and source documents you need to know. As though an examiner might want to hear me defend my life choices or the life I've mapped out for myself, by meandering through the lives of others.

My parents have been dead for some time now – my father in 1989 and my mother in 2014. As happens with the dead, their ghosts populate my thoughts most days, as I question their advice, reflect on the ways they lived. I wish I could conjure them up one more time as Pirandello does his mother in his short story 'Conversation with Mother' and the Tavani brothers' film version of it in *Kaos* (1984). In that story, the Sicilian author called forth his dead mother to tell once again her tale of the family's flight to Malta when she was a teenager. It's clear the story lives for Pirandello but he needs her again as his muse, to tell it one more time, to give his aging memory the illumination it needs to relive her story and through it, his own. Show me how to write your stories, he entreats, show me how to turn the lived memory into words. Shared stories such as these are so potently lived, so enriched, that the past becomes a memory continuum. Why would this not be so when we revisit places as we once did – sometimes with Marcel Proust's intense, involuntary re-enactment, like my experience in the *Jardin des plantes*, and sometimes with a puzzling *déjà vu*, or the familiar comfort of vague sensations, like slipping one's foot into a worn and comfortable shoe.

There are times when I travel in England that I wish my parents were near. I look out the train windows, pointing scenes out to them. I would find their comparisons useful when walking in places they knew, like Royston or Barnsley or the beautiful New Miller Dam with its forest paths and duck-speckled water. These are the places I learned about as a child and as I walk them now, I want to know what has changed and what hasn't. What would they think of Wakefield's Barbara Hepworth Gallery, or the tidily-modern new iteration of Barnsley Market? I can only imagine their responses; and so I write down my observations, my conversations with them across the vast landscapes of death, colouring my writing with what I hope they're telling me. And if not, if what they're really saying is what Ronald Fraser wrote in *The Manor House at Amnersfield, 1933-1945*, 'What actually happened is less important than what is felt to have happened. Is that right?' – then what I have captured of their England must be owned by me alone.

The Vietnam War changed my ideas about Australia and travel. I had joined the protestors at Sydney's anti-war protests while still a teenager, when the country had seared its way onto my formerly Eurocentric world map. I visited Vietnam first in 1994 and went back as a writer almost a decade later, to write about Hanoi and its French colonial history. I have been back numerous times since for writing and research projects. As well as learning about Vietnam's rich history and struggle against colonialism, I also learned a lot about the importance of family. The Vietnamese writers and publishers with whom I worked were always curious about my sense of nation; I'd say I'm Anglo-Australian and sometimes feel torn between the two cultures, and our conversations would inevitably return to the notion of place. For the Vietnamese, I discovered, place is where family is and the two – country and family – are so intertwined it is hard to separate them. There were times when these conversations saddened me. I felt a sense of unbelonging, if that's what it's called. A hollowness where home and country should be located.

Each time I buy a train ticket in England, I feel I am entering a different emotional world. The train will carry me from Lime Street to London or across the Pennines to York or Sheffield or Norwich. Travel is a lonely experience without family. There are too many questions to be asked and conversations to be had. You point out of train windows at the landscape painted on the terrain, in a one-way conversation between a lonely traveller and train and landscape. We loved our train journeys as children, especially those in which my father played the clown. We 'I spied' and gambled on who would see the sea first, pointed at farm animals as though a cow or horse had never been seen before, shared mints and comics bought at the station.

A trip across the north of England is also a trip across the emotional landscape of my childhood. Buying a plane ticket is a different matter altogether. I fly between England and Australia in a nihilistic way. Once I'm in the air the tether of land slips away. Identity becomes unstable in the characterless and homogenised atmosphere of an Airbus or Boeing 777. The crew also seem to belong nowhere. They're chosen for this anationalism, I suspect. They speak multiple languages and are trained to deal with a range of cultural expectations. It is really only when on the ground again that they reassert the airline's national brand – hence the Singapore women in their sarong kabayas or the Emirates staff in their airline's take on a UAE costume. That is what the universality of travel means. You lift off to nothingness and then you claim yourself again when you land. I've often stood at the luggage carousel waiting for my true self to reappear. After 12,000 miles, that battered suitcase full of Englishness that was loaded at Manchester or Heathrow has metamorphosed into an Australian suitcase in the baggage handling area of Kingsford Smith airport. As I wheel it out of the airport and into a taxi, I am a returning Sydneysider welcomed back by my city.

The taxi ride home is also salutary. How did Sydney manage to empty of people in the time I was away? The emptiness, the quiet, the green, the corner shops with their overhanging verandas, the flash of a flock of parrots, the joggers with dogs on leads. I dig into a purse that has Australian money in it, enter a house that has existed without me. The garden has grown more tropical. The frangipani now flowers. My brother knows the drill. He's filled the fridge with vegemite, bread, butter, milk. They will sustain me through a jetlagged hunger at three in the morning. I sleep until midday then head for my favourite café. The owner remembers me though she hasn't seen me in ages. 'Avocado and tomato on toast and a very hot café latte?' She even remembers my usual order.

Sometimes when it is cold and wet in Liverpool, I torture myself with Australian images. The beach, the purple crush of jacaranda flowers on a footpath, Sydney's New Year's Eve fireworks, a Thai meal at an outdoor café with girlfriends. I shuffle these images like playing cards missing an ace or queen. How can I play without the places that exist without me? Will they be there when I go back? Place becomes all about emotions; not just memories, but feelings far more visceral than that. Travelling between them requires a form of shape shifting that allows a smooth passage between letting go and reclaiming.

You stay, you return. It sometimes feels seismic.

CHAPTER SIX
Liverpool

I flew into Liverpool in March 2017 to take up a new job in one of the city's universities. As the plane banked and turned, the sweep of its trajectory took in the countryside of Cheshire, the hills of Wales, the wide and rippling sandbanks of the Mersey, before flying low over the historical village of Hale. As has happened to my landings so many times since, the updraft of currents picked up the plane and danced it around, causing it to dip from side to side as it made its bumpy landing. Along the tarmac the plane rushed, the Mersey visible on my left until it disappeared behind the hillocks that delineate the airport from the grounds of the Tudor manor house, Speke Hall.

Through customs and passport control, I gathered my bags and went out to the taxi rank through the doors of an airport named after one of Liverpool's most famous sons, John Lennon. I had booked temporary accommodation in a serviced apartment in the city centre, and as we drove towards it, I was struck by the arcades of trees that lined the roads, many of them on the verge of bud. There were banks of daffodils too, great rippling swathes of emerging flowers. Then the airport gave way to suburban houses; Edwardian, Victorian, Georgian, some hasty post-war flats. The docks came into view and at the end of them, the Liver Building.

I had seen the docks in the days before they were restored to hold the Tate and the Maritime and Slavery museums. I had passed through them on my first visit to the UK, when I took the Liverpool to Douglas ferry to visit those relatives who lived on the Isle of Man. I didn't stop in Liverpool at that time. I just stepped off the Leeds train at Liverpool's Lime Street station and made my way straight to Pier Head. That visit offered a fleeting vision of a smoggy station and a city stained with the smoke of coal fires and industrial pollution, then a backwards glance at the Liver Building as the Isle of Man ferry headed along the Mersey towards the Irish Sea.

As you wander around the Albert Dock today, you can still hear the flap of ghost sails, catch the fog horns and ships' bells, the multilingual calls of sailors from around the world. From Liverpool's earliest times, shipping has been a major industry and the Mersey a port for international trade. The city remains proud of its status as Britain's second maritime city. All along the Mersey banks, on the western side, the Wirral, and the eastern, Liverpool, are warehouses and wharves and grand buildings that write themselves and their history over the maritime landscape. Many of the buildings once housed the world's most famous shipping lines – White Star, Cunard, Booth – and old photos show the Mersey pulsing with their ships' arrivals and departures, the mucky river water churned with their continuous movement.

Great ships were built and launched on the Mersey, including the *Mauritania* and her sister ship, the *Lusitania*. Liverpool flourished on this maritime prosperity and the spoils that shipping brought; all the products of Empire, from rice and cotton to wool and tea. Live animals too, hence the riverside abattoirs at Birkenhead where sheep and cattle could be off-loaded, straight from ship to butchery. The slave trade brought with it the stain of inhumanity, leaving a dirty fingerprint on imperious architecture built with the profits from the sale of those kidnapped human beings.

The docks were already familiar on my first visit to Liverpool. They'd inveigled their way into our lounge room in Sydney in the northern TV shows of the 1970s like *Z Cars, A Family at War* and also Carla Lane's comedy, *The Liver Birds,* about a couple of young women sharing a flat in the city. In those shows, the Mersey always looked busy and purposeful, with workers scrambling around ships and dry docks. Liverpool was still a working port back then, though that was becoming tenuous, and its docks were still engaged in a maritime conversation with the world. That role ended bitterly in the late 1970s and the 1980s. The jobs went. The docks were decommissioned. Workers were abandoned to unemployment and anger. These days, whenever I visit the museums and cafes in the Albert Dock, the ghosts of the former dock workers seem to haunt the places where once they'd earned a living. Their sons and daughters take their own children to see what once fed, housed and clothed them, like visitors to a theme park dedicated to deindustrialization.

The Albert Dock and the area that surrounds it is now a UNESCO World Heritage site and a major tourist attraction. You can see why. Thousands of jobs may have been lost, the shipping and containerization gone further up the river to Bootle, but these docks remain unique and beautiful in their reincarnation. They sing their history, the Mersey lapping and humming along. The deep dry docks, now ship-less and filled with dark green water, reflect the thrust and shape of industrial architecture. The museums offer the voices of slaves and workers and sailors long gone. It is the perfect exemplar of English nostalgia; a historical site that celebrates not just the lost world of work but also the mournful historicization of it through museums and re-enactments.

Once I had settled into my apartment, I wandered around the city. Like most contemporary cities, Liverpool has a pedestrianized shopping street lined with the usual British chain stores. From time to time I would stop and look up, surprised by a sudden façade or architectural detail. The Bluecoat building, which dates back to 1716. The nearby Athenaeum Club, a beautifully-detailed Georgian shop front in Mount Pleasant. The 'bombed-out church,' a shell now and left as it stood when almost flattened in the great German blitz of 1940/41.

Accompanying my walk were the raucous and shrill calls of herring gulls, soaring overhead. People in Liverpool call to one another too – it is a loud place, where people seem to unselfconsciously share their conversations with everyone around them. They chat to you out of the blue, as well. On buses, in shops, on benches. More than any other English city, Liverpool reminds me of Australia in that regard. All of the conversations are enhanced by the curious accent, its cadences and jargon, perplexing and at times incomprehensible. So strong was the accent of a man who worked at one of my university's cafes, I presumed he was from Eastern Europe until he told me his family had lived in Lark Lane for six generations.

The scouse accent, I would slowly learn as my ear calibrated to the suburbs, north and south, has a number of sub accents, though initially it seemed a homogenized blur, all 'wares' and 'y'rihts?' This linguistic discovery was a two-way exchange. As soon as I opened my mouth and people heard my Australian accent I faced a barrage of questions: Are you here on holidays? Where are you from in Australia? When I explained I'd come to Liverpool to live and work for a while, the inevitable question was 'whatever for?' though this was often quickly followed with 'so what do you think of our city?' Taxi drivers, shop assistants, strangers on buses, academics, students – there is a cousin or daughter or brother or long-lost school friend who lives in Australia, somewhere. Years have passed since those first explorations and I am still asked these questions most days.

The curiosity is both oppressive and welcome, but it is also loaded with an awful privilege. I haven't witnessed much overt racism yet in Liverpool, but I wonder whether such questions of national origin are asked of the city's Somalian or Yemini immigrants. I'm white; I pose no perceived threat. I may have come here for work, but it is the kind of work most people don't do. That I paid my own way is inherent in my acceptance by the locals, so I am not seen as a sponger. Relatives in Australia, in Elizabeth, Brisbane or Melbourne, mean we have people in common in a white, English speaking, former colony, which means I'm one of them.

On the way to my apartment the taxi driver passed the grand maritime buildings in The Strand, Duke Street with its boarded-up Georgian townhouses, the green, gold and red gates of Chinatown. *I'm going to be living in the North*, I thought, a frisson of new ownership colouring all that I observed. I may have been reclaiming some of my family's Yorkshire Northernness, but the north means different things to different people, I would discover, as not all Liverpudlians see themselves as 'northern'. Michael Swerdlow, for one. He was quoted in Stuart Maconie's book, *Pies and Prejudice*, declaring 'What have I got in common with Newcastle or Yorkshire or the Lake District? What I am is Liverpudlian.' As I read that I thought of my parents and the Northernness they carried to Australia on the *Empire Brent* like a specially-packed suitcase, like a family heirloom to pass down the generations. Their regionality was both a blessing and a curse, a cloak that they just couldn't or wouldn't shake off. Yorkshireness differentiated it, I suppose, from the wider meaning of being from the north. Their identities were specific to Yorkshire, and in particular, their little part of it, which also encompassed the small villages dotted between Wakefield, Royston and Barnsley – Havercroft, Shafton, Featherstone, Ryhill – names that didn't mean much until I visited them from Liverpool. I heard my parents' voices all around me though, like some kind of Yorkshire syren's call. I caught a glimpse of my father in every man in a flat cap and my mother in that slow Yorkshire drawl that seemed both self-effacing and challenging at the same time. *God*, I thought, with a sentimental thump of my heart – *I could just as well be back in Bankstown.*

Swerdlow's declaration of his identity as Liverpudlian, first and foremost, has come to mean more now I've lived here a while. I'm understanding better the different areas of the city and the types of people who are perceived to live in them, and what that means for self-definitions within a place. For example, the street in which I currently live in the city's 'Georgian Quarter' houses academics from three of the city's four universities, University of Liverpool, Liverpool Hope and Liverpool John Moores, as well as Edge Hill in nearby Ormskirk. Once, the Georgian Quarter was the city's red light district and, I'm told gleefully, you could pick up the now expensive Georgian houses for a song. One of Liverpool's most famous poets, the late Adrian Henri, used to live a few doors away, so I also hear stories of parties and poetry nights when writers, academics and an assorted mob of literary 'scallys' would collect to celebrate and argue about politics and poetics. Nearby Toxteth is famous for the riots of 1985, when the area erupted with rage and frustration about the Tory government's vicious austerity policies.

It still houses a diverse community of old and newer migrants from the Middle East and North Africa. Granby Street has halal butchers and cake shops that sell baklava, and nearby there is a mosque, a Greek church and a synagogue. This diversity spills into the streets at the monthly Granby Street market with its ethnic music and food.

Aigburth in the south is a suburb full of writers, students and artists. Its streets bleed into the wide, green expanses of Sefton Park, an area as vast as London's Hyde Park. On any sunlit Sunday, the park teems with families and people walking their dogs. I hang about there too, afterwards heading for coffee and cake at one of the cafés in nearby Lark Lane. The suburbs of the Wirral, across the river, have a Cheshire postcode and that makes them unable to claim a Liverpool pedigree – at least, that's the view of the numerous taxi drivers with whom I've discussed the city. One thing becomes clear in any discussions about Liverpool with the locals: they guard the place and its reputation against any criticism or attack, and they expect incomers like me to do the same.

This love of birthplace has found its way into books and poems and plays by local authors. 'This city is my muse,' writes Liverpool writer and academic, Jeff Young, in his plangent tribute to his Liverpool, *Ghost Town*:

> Its unruliness and awkwardness, its rebellious spirit, its ugliness and beauty filter into the stories I write and make the work wayward and disruptive. I have written characters inspired by the particular atmospheres of certain back alleys and ruined buildings. I have tried to imbue a story with the melancholy beauty of Liverpool's psychedelic sunsets. I had the feeling – still have the feeling – that the city was a living novel and we were walking through its pages.

There is a religiosity within this ordination to place. Liverpool is like a wafer on the end of a tongue. Movement through it seems incantatory and biblical in its parables and sermons. The city and its people have been beaten down, bombed, starved, mocked and blamed. It has met the indifference of politicians and civil servants with a kind of scouse bravado that often masks a deeper and more existential despair. In these ways, Liverpool is seen as a city unique in the UK. It gets up, punch drunk, and soldiers on, yet its sophistication and outward-looking character led it to vote remain in the 2016 EU referendum. It also returns Labour candidates by the largest margin in the country – around 85% at general and local elections. People have doggedly fought for justice for the victims of the Hillsborough stadium disaster and the reputation of its media-vilified football fans. Liverpool has also delivered some of the UK's most exciting arts festivals. It is innovative, artistic, culturally proud, welcoming. If the biblical Job had paired his capacity for long-suffering with the jaw-grip of a bull terrier, I suspect you'd have a sense of the deeply tribal and tough people I'm writing about.

These qualities and characteristics mean that Liverpool is often in the British news, recently with the Mayor being arrested and the city council suspended and replaced with administrators, but the city's character hasn't always endeared Liverpudlians to people in other parts of England. The city seems to have suffered the same types of negative stereotypes that bedevil any definitive characterizing of place. Scousers can be seen as complaining, aggressive ne'r-do-wells by some; when I announced my new job to friends from England's south I was met with bemusement of the 'what do you want to live up *there* for' kind. I don't think I'd have received the same reaction about York, Leeds or

Manchester. Liverpool, in the eyes of conservatives from the south, is a city full of rogues and complainers, England's own local version of Australia's 'whinging Poms.' Liverpool's critics include the former Prime Minister, Boris Johnson, who, when writing for *The Spectator* in the days before his Prime-ministerial role, made the mistake of declaring that Liverpudlians, 'see themselves whenever possible as victims, and resent their victim status; yet at the same time wallow in it.' Others have added their views to this litany: the Yorkshire writer Alan Bennett referred to Liverpudlians' 'built-in air of grievance', and the former Chief Executive of Liverpool Council, Sir David Henshaw, reflected sadly that Liverpool was 'the most mind-bogglingly awful and whinging place, where the glass is always half-empty.'

Whenever I have discussed these reactions with friends whose history in the city goes back generations, I'm usually met with a philosophical shrug. 'There are scallys everywhere, Cath,' or words to that effect. Jeff Young is a case in point. His family's relationship with the city is visceral – its challenge might as well be, 'you hurt another Liverpudlian, you hurt me.' This also applies to the city's buildings and the history and lives that are enmeshed in them. 'My grandfather,' Young writes in *Ghost Town*:

had a map inside his heart of the city he had lived in all his life. He couldn't hear the bulldozers, couldn't see the houses falling. He would walk along the desolate wasteland streets, his inner compass guiding him past the ghosts of vanished terraced houses, corner shops, alehouses, the butcher's and the baker's. There was nothing to the left, nothing to the right, nothing on any of the four horizons except for debris and rubble. The cobbled streets still framed the emptiness, but there was no one left to walk through the frames, no photographer to capture the city as it once was. Just granddad walking through a city which is no longer there.

What might I have written about my family's generational relationship with Yorkshire had my parents stayed in Royston? Something of Royston's history and loss? Migration sweeps this cross-generational ownership of a place from you, those ghosts with whom writers like Jeff Young share their daily lives. When I walk in Royston or Barnsley these days, it is with a camera and notebook. I am hungry for clues about what my people might have done there, but their ghosts are too far removed to make themselves visible; perhaps that is the revenge of the ghosts that migration leaves behind. Miffed by abandonment, they don't come when you call them.

At least I can summon a real pride in Liverpool whenever friends from Australia or France come to visit. We wander the tourist places together, and I take them to the 'secret' places I've discovered on my rambles. It's not the same as showing people a place with which you're intimate; more a tour with a shallowly-planted newcomer. As I show off the battler city – the sad, boarded up terrace houses in Wavertree, the Georgian opulence of Faulkner Street, the cheery market in Great Homer Street – I feel a joy in sharing it with others. 'Isn't it interesting?' I ask, like some over-excited antipodean anthropologist. 'Have you ever seen anything like it?' Questions no doubt posed by the millions of visitors to Liverpool since the city was made a UNESCO Capital of Culture in 2009, a role that has fed cultural tourism ever since.

Like other migrants in other places, I have greedily experienced the city in all possible ways, collecting suggestions for outings from locals in the know. I visit Great Homer Street Market on Saturdays for the cheap plants and vegetables, the stalls full of out-of-season clothes or goods that may have fallen off the back of a truck. A close friend's father once ran a stall in the market, so each visit prompts questions of culture and place. The market stallholders engage in a banter that seems to be a skill in markets around the world. You can't buy anything without trading a conversation about its relative merits, colour or style. I present myself as an oddity, my Australian accent immediately inviting comment. There are the inevitable stallholders or customers with cousins in Sydney and Perth, or someone planning a trip to Queensland and wanting hotel recommendations.

I walk in Sefton Park, in Princes Park, great spread-out reams of parkland, ponds, crocuses and daffodils in spring. I wander along the river or cross to the Wirral and walk to New Brighton, catching a train home through the Mersey Tunnel. I haunt the Tate and the Walker Galleries. Pace the Welsh Streets and look for the house in which Ringo Starr was born. Liverpool is discovered by the soles of my feet – it is exactly the opposite of what Susannah Radstone's friend described in his criticism of Australia's lack of history for non-indigenous Australians. In Liverpool it is there in strata after strata.

Settling into Liverpool has made me painfully aware of what my parents went through. It is one thing to work in a different Australian city, to fly home on Friday afternoons and return to my university on Monday morning; it is quite another to move countries. As I reconcile myself to loneliness, bad weather, class and conservatism, I can only applaud again the courage my parents showed in their move. I am learning a great deal about isolation, alienation and homesickness, and reflecting with more sympathy on the way in which they tackled these feelings as they calibrated themselves to their new life in Sydney. They were brave and determined and stubborn and grateful, all qualities it took me a long time to acknowledge.

I ask colleagues, students and friends who were born overseas how they washed up on the shores of the Mersey. Like me, some came for academic jobs, some for study, others came as tourists for adventure and stayed. Like James Woods, some feel their migration was accidental and they may move on again – one day. Sharing stories with other migrants opens up points of comparison and loss; what we miss about our homeland, what we love about this new one. A colleague from Latvia is teetering on the edge of going home. Just after Brexit she began to notice changes in people's attitudes to her accent. She is worried that England no longer feels like her new home. A fellow Australian is relishing the adventure. There's no time limit on it – yet – but she will go home. This escape option is what makes living here both a blessing and a curse. On the one hand, I feel settled in and excited by my new life; on the other, the option of return stops me from feeling too tethered to place. That tethering seems the key to fully immersing yourself in the new country. Knowing you can't go back must surely make you work harder to make a go of it. I can just 'cut and run' if I become too fed up. I have the privilege of belonging in two places at once, and locating myself in whichever one feels most like home.

I fear I may not have the same stamina to remain in Britain as my parents displayed in their migration to Australia. There are days when I long for the relationships shared with friends of long standing, the similar cultural markers and styles of humour, the easy lifestyle of a beach or a big, wide garden. England feels too small and contained, too interior.

I still ask my parents about this as I negotiate my own passage from one country to another, hoping their spirits can offer some advice. Migration takes a lot more negotiation than people realise. You're curious, so you want to ask lots of questions of people who don't particularly want to answer them. We have our own interior road maps and they don't always follow the same metrics. In Australia, I think nothing of a two-hour train journey – I might just be reaching the outskirts of Sydney in that time – yet the 40 minutes between Liverpool and Manchester or the two hours to Leeds can seem like a major journey, and a significant cost. How do you explain these matters of dimension? On my office wall I have put a map of Australia superimposed over one of Europe. Australia stretches from the UK to Turkey, from Morocco to Finland.

My scorn for parents who rarely left their patch in Yorkshire before departing on their 12,000 mile migration is cast into a new light now. I haven't ventured all that far either; to London, Norwich, York, Glasgow, Leeds and Sheffield, but to far fewer places that I imagined I would. It is the cost, in part – I find it incomprehensible that you need to book a train so far ahead to get a good price for a day out to a beach – and then what happens if it's raining? Trains can be cancelled at short notice and with no apology. It all just feels like too much trouble.

My reluctance to travel in England may also be in part because Liverpool continues to enthral me. Why go to Bath when Liverpool has more Georgian architecture than any British city, other than London? The pubs, theatre, music and art are second to none. There are rituals to establish – a Saturday trek to Great Homer Street Market, a lazy late lunch, a walk, a film at FACT, a meal in one of the city's great restaurants. Sunday exploring the beaches of the Wirral, or those to be found where the Mersey runs into the sea. There's a lifetime of exploration to be undertaken, and I am new to it with much to learn. The city is also in a constant state of flux as new buildings rise or old ones are renovated. A set of doors, a façade, may be gone the next time I pass by them. At times, places seem as fluid as my explorations, a city shifting and sliding as its history disappears.

Homesickness sometimes punctuates my explorations of the city. There are days when my skin seems to beg for the feel of sand and sun and sea. I wander off into a nostalgic fugue. I am on Austinmer Beach and about to plunge into the sea pool. If I float on my back I can regard the outline of the Illawarra escarpment, those great sandstone cliffs that rise up beyond the beach, forming a narrow corridor between escarpment and road and shops and sand. The ancient sandstone is worn in parts, and the newly-exposed sections throw gold across a cliff face which is also host to gum trees dotted with the screeching white shapes of sulphur-crested cockatoos. The birds fly down to the Norfolk pines that line the beach front – gossiping and screeching and showering the picnickers below them with pine nuts. Instead, I have learned to enjoy Liverpool's wildlife. My garden is visited by a Robin redbreast – those harbingers of Christmas on the cards we received from England. The little bird is quieter than its Australian cousins, but it is friendly enough.

Being homesick in Liverpool casts a new light on what my parents felt in Sydney, my mother especially. She wasn't a woman who expressed her feelings very actively. Her homesickness seemed to dissolve into a constant state of busyness. She was forever sewing and gardening and painting and cooking. She wasn't someone you could ask questions of, not in those early years anyway, when, as I understand now, her homesickness was too raw to expose to scrutiny. This reluctance to talk means her inner world remains closed, and more mysterious to me. Her life feels less lived. She is like Penelope sewing and waiting, in my mother's case not for Ulysses but for some revelation, some messenger who will confirm that she made the right decision. Before she aged into dementia and her memories were swept away for good, we did manage to chat about those early years, the decision to leave England, the voyage, the building of the house in Bankstown and the settlement into the new life. Despite the decades that had passed since she arrived in Sydney, she remained true to the mantra – we did it for you kids. But what about YOU, I asked. What about what *you* needed?

Her Yorkshire pragmatism would kick in at this stage, after a lifetime of saying the same words over and over again – *what's the point, what's done is done, we did it for you kids, you won't get compliments from Coles, you made your bed and you lie in it, don't look back* – I could fill a book with them. Any regrets were neatly stitched into her secret, private life and there they remained; no questions, no answers, just the family line of being grateful that they did what they did for us. I *am* grateful. Without their migration I might not be here today, in Liverpool, in a university; a woman with the freedom to travel and work, to see the world from north and south, inside and out, to explore the ways in which travel has broadened our family in some ways and narrowed us in others.

In Liverpool, these thoughts tumble around me like squealing, wayward children on one of those Australian beach holidays. Carelessly unchallenged, chiding against, picking at something that should be left alone. They also assert, as Ghasan Hage has done, that we should stop seeing migration as a tragic story about the loss of a homeland.

There are happy times to be remembered and shared. In the collective memory of migration and the new homeland rests the triumphal marches of courage, resilience and happiness regained.

I received an email from a former postgraduate student in Sydney. She wanted to catch up and was surprised to hear I was living in Liverpool. She once lived in Liverpool too, a few streets away, in the 1980s. Toxteth. She was there when the riots convulsed the city. We didn't ever have this conversation in Sydney so I'm surprised we are having it now. 'Who would have guessed', I write. 'What a small world.' I am slipping into my parents' aphoristic way of talking, and the realization is far from comfortable. Perhaps there is an aphorism, a truism, a time and place for everything? A conversation that couldn't be had during an MA supervision is made all the richer by having it now, *in situ*, as we share images of her former city, now mine. The long twilights, the pinkening sky making chess pieces of a thrust of chimneys, the sound of car tires on cobblestones, the cathedral bells, the persistent smell of long extinguished coal fires, the seagulls, the Mersey ferry, the pubs where your youthful self is forever propping up the bar, the sheen of wet cobbles, the foghorn that rises up from the river like an admonishment. 'Yes,' I say, 'oh yes. It's all still here.' New for me though, old for you, a city that refracts and spins and shapeshifts like a kaleidoscope offering a new way of seeing itself with each turn of the tube.

Being in Liverpool also means I live relatively close to my family's old stomping grounds in Yorkshire. I don't have a car so I go to Yorkshire by train. There are two ways to get there. One, Liverpool to Sheffield, takes me across the Derby Peak District, a rolling landscape bifurcated with low stone fences and hills and fells. That train ambles around the north and midlands of England on its way to Norwich, and the first leg, to Sheffield, offers glimpses of Peak District villages and places to alight for a ramble. I change at Sheffield for the Barnsley train, waiting on the platform under Sheffield's station roof, another of the northern stations that built the swagger of industrial prosperity into its architecture. There I wait below the cast iron and glass and courting pigeons for the humbler Sheffield to Wakefield branch-line train. The Sheffield accent reels me home. The bemusement too, when I display my own accent as I ask for directions or a timetable update, or buy a coffee from one of the platform's ubiquitous café chains.

Sheffield was once famous for its steel industry, for the city's coal-blackened buildings and its accent, which is seen as one of Yorkshire's most incomprehensible. On the Barnsley train I look out at sidings covered in cow parsley and buddleia, watch a man who could be a ghost of my father on his old Raleigh bike, cycling somewhere in his tweed cloth cap and the Fair Isle jersey his mother lovingly knitted for her sugar baby son. Dark brown, yellow and white, the stitches impossibly neat and interwoven; she might just as well have been knitting him into her body, the wool holding on to him. That pullover is run to holes now, but I still have it in a trunk in Sydney.

Barnsley has an impressive town hall library and museum, in which I research old family and wander about a display of relics from the past – miners' gear, tea sets, cinema posters, football paraphernalia from that wonder time when Barnsley Football Club won the FA Cup. I follow my father's ghost into Barnsley market, so like the Paddy's market of Sydney and with the same cantankerous stall holders my Great Aunt Kate bartered with as my boy-father watched nervously and shuffled his feet. Barnsley is a city that displays its history through the defiant bravado of poverty. It has some of the worst unemployment in the North of England and voted for Brexit in the 2016 EU referendum. I'm not here for that though, not here for the struggles of others. My father was here and that's who I'm looking for, his boy-self, potato-knee-ed and toothy; his gangly, shy teenage self on his bike, his outings to the pictures with my mother, too shy to kiss her for months after their first date. I'm in Barnsley because my father took Barnsley with him to Sydney and I'm here to bring something of it back.

Like Sydney, Liverpool is defined by water. The Mersey has known stories of arrival and departure, its waters sweeping them along like a great tidal broom. Pier Head was the stepping-off point into Liverpool for Irish escaping the Great Famine. Most of that suffering, starved throng disembarked from the steam packets that carried them from Belfast or Dublin to a life of further penury in England. When you read the newspaper articles of the time about these desperate Irish immigrants, the reportage is striking in its similarity to the tirades we read today in the UK's conservative tabloids about Syrians or Yemeni or Somalian refugees. While many Irish migrants continued on to the USA or British colonies, thousands stayed, and you see the faces of their descendants on Liverpool's streets – Irish faces, blue eyes, dark hair or gingerly Celtic – and you hear them too in the complex rhythms of scouse and the city's linguistic poetics.

The Scots and Welsh came as well, Welsh masons and craftsmen playing a key role in Liverpool's architecture. They're celebrated in the streets around the 'Welsh Streets' of Toxteth in street names like Powis and Gwydir and Pengwern and in the now derelict Welsh Church on Princes

Road. Sailors came and went, some staying in the city. Luminaries came – Lytton Strachey, the Egyptian/Greek poet, Cavafy, as a child, de Quincy, Gerard Manley Hopkins, Joseph Conrad, the French pioneering filmmakers, the Lumiere brothers, who filmed the docks in 1901. It is home to two of the world's greatest football teams, a cultural hub, a musical watershed. It is the second most popular tourist destination in the UK. No wonder the city is also known for its pride and pugnacity – its Liverpool exceptionalism.

Liverpool is a city of departures too. Of exiles. Thousands of slaves, carted off to the colonies, to the sugar fields of the Caribbean; west, east, all those fearful, febrile dreams sailing along like ghost ships. Awaiting God-knows-what life when they landed, despairing of getting ill and being turfed overboard. Lines of men and women in chains. You see their ghostly imprints on the buildings that run down to the river or in the colonial names – 'Africa House', 'India House', the stone-carved open-mouthed lions of colonial power, the nymphs and sprites and Neptunes above a window, and there on the skyline, the flightless Liver Birds watching the ships come and go.

Liverpudlians sailed away to other countries too – to the USA, Australia, Canada, Rhodesia, New Zealand. To trace a finger along a shipping list is to trace emigrants shedding their skins. This flux is Liverpool's narrative. Framed prints of old shipping posters decorate the walls of a pub in Duke Street. After the Titanic's sinking, these great ships still held their attraction. Six days to New York, three weeks to Colombo, five weeks to Sydney. Liverpool, a city from which the shipping news radiated sea maps in knots and nautical miles.

People ask when I'll leave, and whenever they do I suspect that Liverpool is also a city worried about abandonment –

that it sometimes thinks its role is to just watch everyone go from the docks in Birkenhead or Pier Head. The famous, getting away as quickly as they can. It is always a surprise to hear an actor or celebrity came from Liverpool. Really? They don't *sound* as though they did, having 'ditched the accent'. I once heard some academics talking about the regions of England with the worst accents – Liverpool was amongst them – and the need for people to obliterate their accent if they wanted to get on. The conversation seemed shameful and deeply classist, but there it was; normalised, expected. Scouse, a stain on an academic CV.

Liverpudlians know that in ditching the accent they also ditch a class that spoke of hunger; of a roughness born of a childhood playing in the bomb craters that still pockmarked the city well into the 1970s. The Toxteth riots. Hillsborough. Heysel. Unemployment and poverty. Fleeing the cruel and indifferent iron hand of devolution and deindustrialization. Escaping Conservative economic policies designed to humiliate people into behaving themselves. Regeneration that meant the docks became a cultural site of a shipping history without workers or ships. Leaving. Departure is perhaps this city's proper name.

From my very first walk, it was Liverpool's maritime history that enchanted me the most. Whenever I walk along the Mersey and around the docks they still speak to me of my own family's relationship with the sea. I can feel the pull of the ships, the reverberations of the *Empire Brent's* departure from Glasgow with my family on board. Millions of people in this city have been associated with ships and the sea from generation to generation. Britain may be a maritime nation, and nowhere in Britain has a maritime history quite like Liverpool. The Mersey is so wide in parts it resembles

Sydney harbour. I always feel a frisson of familiarity, a link with Sydney, when I walk by the Mersey. From the promenade in front of the Three Graces buildings, I can stand at the railings and watch the Mersey ferry make a slow turn from Birkenhead to the ferry terminal. The water at dusk is particularly evocative of Sydney. It catches spangles of light as the sun dips. I could be standing at the rails of Sydney's Circular Quay.

Memories hijack like this in the strangest ways. Walking along Lime Street, I'm drawn into a scent, a sound, into potent sensory fugues. Sydney has certain unique smells that hardly seem to change. They hang around the city's streets like the cooked cabbage of a century-old meal. There's the harbour smell that rises up from Circular Quay, spreading salt and seaweed through the city. It's particularly noticeable on summer evenings when the leaving of an air-conditioned building becomes a reunion with every visit to the beach, the twilight ozone defying the fog of car fumes.

I wish my parents were still alive so I could discuss these thoughts with them. Their departure infected our lives in Australia, after all. They departed. They knew the drill. The packing, farewell, the ship, the sea, the new place. The touch of it stalking each new experience in the new place. It is like a watermark in most of the books and poetry I've written. Someone in each of them is about to step off somewhere. 'Departure is always pieces of sky, land, water, a rickety gangplank above concrete bollards and straining ropes,' I wrote in one poem, and in another, 'Departure unscales the eyes to the body's frailties and each crease of time.' Departure has cast its shadow over our lives and the lives of millions of other migrant families. It is like those pernicious religious rumours of original sin. Inescapable, historical. A city like Liverpool can feel blighted by it, as its inhabitants turn always to the water, to the current, the sandbanks and river mouth drawing the ships towards the sea and away. I suspect it has stained the lives of Liverpudlians in the same way – their relatives left, their fathers worked in the docks or went to sea. Those who stayed dreamed their own dreams of escape as they watched the other passengers come and go.

Until I moved to Liverpool all my previous visits to the UK had been holidays, sometimes long ones like the year I back-packed or rode my moped around the British Isles, or short four-weeks-at-a-time stays when my partner and I hired a cottage and a car and travelled out from carefully-selected picturesque villages and towns. We rented apartments in London too, posh places in Chelsea or Knightsbridge, places we could never afford to buy but which offered a holiday week of luxurious proximity to Harrod's food hall or Harvey Nichols, a fantasy life where prosperous London was ours.

Liverpool opened up new possibilities. It was next door to Yorkshire for a start, and from Lime Street Station I expect-ed to make regular forays into my parents' old lives; though I'm still not sure what emotional revelations I was expecting from my move to Liverpool. I'd already plundered England and my family memories of Yorkshire, so there was nothing I felt would surprise me in Merseyside. As a young wom-an, I'd travelled Yorkshire, scooping up the family stories, matching them with what I'd heard in Sydney, gluing the two together. I felt this process had provided me with a comprehensive picture – one layered with both subtlety and emphasis. Things now made sense that had confused me since I was a child. Perplexity was stripped bare, and in its place stood a greater sense of my dual identity.

Like the researcher of *Ten Pound Poms*, Alistair Thomson, whose Australian accent also prompted conversations with people in Britain about relatives in Australia, the questions the people of Liverpool asked me led to further questioning of myself. Like Thomson, I found myself often being reminded 'of aspects of (my) own, unintended migration: for example, the acute homesickness of the first years in England; an undiminished longing for the landscape and seascape of eastern Australia; and the practical difficulties of living in a transnational extended family.'

With each new cultural encounter, with each nuance of class or colonialism, the gendered workplace, the jokes about Australia, the inevitable feeling of being too far from those I love, I reflected, questioned, regretted or was exhilarated by the steps I'd taken. These emotions combined into something like homesickness – manifesting itself in an otherworldliness in which each new experience needed to be calibrated against my parents' experiences as migrants and the consequences of them from which I'd sprung.

These emotions made for an uncomfortable transition into the UK. I live here for the moment, but I can terminate the relationship at any time. I can go home because I have a home in Australia to go home to. I can stay here because I have a British passport and a senior job in a university, and my Georgian house is a five-minute walk away from work and all the city's attractions. If my parents were alive, I am sure they'd be proud of and impressed by these privileges. How lucky am I, I would ask, to be able to travel, live and work with such an abundance of choice? Stay, go, work, return. Escape the winter cold or the summer heat. Participate in the cultures of the two countries that shaped who I am. Curse or rail against either as a local.

My parents didn't share this privilege because they were the ones who gave up their own Yorkshire community to forge this duality for their children. They left England as working-class people and that they remained, but their actions provided us with the foundations we needed to become middle class: education, housing, stocks and shares, superannuation, travel, occupations in the civil service or universities. These opportunities were harnessed to our dual identities. We were Australian and British and we had the passports to prove it. The closing of opportunities for working-class Britons to migrate to countries like Australia or Canada may offer some insight into the hostility so many felt when voting in the European Union referendum of 2016 and the 2019 General Election. In both, people seemed to vote against their own best economic interests. They can no longer take advantage of migration opportunities such as people did in the years just after World War II. They are trapped in the once-proud and industrious Midlands and northern communities that now have nothing to offer them. No industries. No skilled jobs. There is anger and resentment at the feeling that others benefit from travel or work opportunities that they can never access. For Britons who have felt trapped by economically-depressed communities and the barriers of class and education, migration has become a loaded term as the review of Peter Gatrell's book, *The Unsettling of Europe* asserts. Migration now represents:

the short-termist and sometimes callous policies of governments who treat migrant workers as a means to an end, the hostility and racism that people moving around Europe have often encountered, and the periodic imposition of border controls that push people to hire smugglers, or risk their lives, to get where they feel they need to.

Why not vote, then, for promises of a return to those days when England led the world in manufacturing?

Freedom of movement. As the UK prepared to leave the European Union one could only wonder why anyone would want to give up such a liberty. Perhaps it was because they didn't feel they had any freedom to lose. Thanks to post-war migration policies, my parents were able to give their children Australia and the UK and for that I am supremely grateful. In 2018 the former British Prime Minister, Theresa May, referred to people who wanted to maintain their access to Europe as 'citizens of nowhere'. It's a particularly insensitive term, especially given the UK's hostility to migrants and refugees and the appalling treatment of groups like the Windrush generation. But May wasn't referring to those groups – she was talking about people like me, who are thankful for the multiple identities we have, not grounded in place or nationalistic in the traditional gung-ho ways, but rather fluid and with access to large parts of the world.

During my first six months, I explored Liverpool, taking photographs of all the city's details, those tiny and surprising moments when I came upon a frieze or a doorway or a portico emblazoned with the city's history. I photographed the Mersey from the ferry, recorded hidden places that not many locals seemed to know. The world of the migrant must be formed from these polarities and perspectives, the tiny details – the wider vistas – the seductiveness of the new tempered with the loss of the old. Eventually the focus shifts. Familiarity with the new place causes the shine to tarnish as the tiny details merge, then disappear. You become a local though you really aren't, because your accent and cultural markings make it too clear to those who have keen ears and eyes for the cadences of generations in one place. You will always be treated as other.

This idea of generational ownership still fills me with wonder. Someone's ancestors lived here for how long? For indigenous Australians this connection to the land goes back thousands of years – so far back for so long they wear the landscape in their blood and bones and skin. Denying this is a thief's game, a thief who came from somewhere else and stole the land. It is why migrant Australians are so much in denial about the country. You might claim it, but it isn't really yours. Each part of the landscape is revered by the original owners. It's theirs.

Coming back to England offers a different kind of claim, a reverse claim on place. Not Yorkshire, Barnsley, Royston – too much has changed in those places for me to lay a claim to them – but in England generally, and the nebulous qualities that being in England shape in me, like a plucked string, like a chord from an old song, a whiff on a breeze, something salty or sweet on the tip of my tongue.

In meetings at the city council which are held in a building beside the Mersey, I watch the dazzle ship, the Mersey ferry, slowly criss-cross the river. A three-hour meeting offers a number of departures and returns, the ferry's dazzling geometric coat of red and yellow and black and blue adding a splash of colour to the grey sky and water. I can see down into the apartments in the building below too – one of those new modern buildings that have caused UNESCO some angst about why they are being allowed to encroach on the colonial grandeur of the riverside. While this kind of incursion is hotly debated in the city, the council also spends time ensuring its historical quarters are maintained. My street was recently re-cobbled, the modern streetlights replaced by some in the style of Georgian gas lights. The houses in the aforementioned 'Welsh Streets' are being restored and filled with young families and artists, bringing new energy into an area that had degenerated into poverty during the Thatcher years.

With each new discovery, I feel more torn. Despite my annual return to Sydney to visit family, Liverpool is beginning to feel strangely like home. I resist this new sense of belonging in a new place. Did my parents feel this when they began to settle in Sydney? Were the ties to the old place stretching and straining? I worry that I'll give up my Australian home – all the people and places I miss – and replace them with a new set of friends and geography. The dazzle ship will become the Balmain ferry, my mapping of its journey as it crosses the Mersey replacing the exhilaration of crossing Sydney Harbour, under the harbour bridge and alighting at Yeroulbin Point. That climb up the stone stairs of Yeroulbin Park, that last turn to watch the ferry scoot towards Greenwich and a last look at the Harbour Bridge and the yachts before walking home. My parents must have some answers. Did you feel this about Royston? Did you long for the sound of the pit bell announcing the end of a shift? The smell of coal in a grate? The sugar pigs? Your mother's parkin? 'They recede,' they call from wherever their spirits rest now – 'time makes them fade.'

Herring gulls call to one another throughout the Liverpool night. They have colonised Liverpool's riverside and suburbs. Superstition says they're the souls of drowned sailors, calling from underwater to the living on the land. Raucous, they scream from buildings, across the city's wharves and the stretch of treacherous water that is the Mersey. Wide of wing, the young are as speckled and brown as hens' eggs, the older birds aggressive and wayward. I hear them in the middle of the night, feel the low-flying flash as one streaks after some thrown food, catch a glimpse of an under-wing as I walk to work, far up in the sky, barely visible against a dapple of clouds. The gulls follow the ships, just until the river meets the sea, then they turn landward again; pretend albatrosses, wing tips tingling in the slipstream.

One day, as I traced Liverpool's maritime history at the Mersey Maritime Museum, I finally discovered a Liverpool connection that tied the *Empire Brent* to Merseyside as potently as if she was moored outside the museum at Pier Head. It was a day misty with rain, the sort that throws a veil over your view of the world. History creeps towards you like a fret over water. As I looked out of the museum's windows, I imagined the port of Liverpool as it was in the city's industrial and maritime heyday. The docks were bristling with cranes. Ships were lined up from New Brighton on the Wirral to Crosby at the north of Liverpool. The maritime industries, warehouses, abattoirs and tanneries, were full of men. Through a wintery mist on 20 November 1946, the *Empire Brent* made a fateful progression down the Mersey. She was in Liverpool under a commission between the British and Canadian governments to take 381 war brides and their children to a new life in Canada.

As she made her way towards the Mersey mouth and the Irish Sea, she was approached by the *Stormont*, an Irish provision ship that was loaded with cattle, horses and a pony, vegetables and food. The two ships collided not far from the Albert Dock, awakening the war brides who were still asleep in their cabins. The *Empire Brent* sustained damage to her prow above the water line but the *Stormont* was a far smaller ship and began taking on water. Her crew was rescued and an attempt was made to save the ship and her cargo, but she overbalanced and ran aground on Pluckington Bank, the notorious Mersey sandbar that has claimed the lives of numerous seamen and ships. At low tide, the bank stretches across the river, a bane to Mersey shipping.

Most of the animals drowned; some washed ashore as far afield as Blackpool and Douglas on the Isle of Man or were killed by abattoir workers brought over from Birkenhead to undertake mercy killings. Some cattle swam away, were lassoed and captured in the water near the Albert Dock and lifted, by crane, onto the docks. The horses drowned too but the pony survived. It was the property of a horse dealer, Mr Rabinowicz of Lark Lane, and had been bought for the Chester Hunt. Today, the Lark Lane stables house a funeral parlour. A lengthy battle began about the pony's true worth once the salvage company began dispersing the salvaged goods.

The Ministry of Food (Potatoes and Carrots Section) was responsible for assessing the worth of the salvaged fruit and vegetables, while the tins of powdered milk were the responsibility of the Ministry's Salvaged Foods Section. For months, the port of Liverpool negotiated its way through the red tape required in a time of strict rationing. The *Stormont* was broken up, and her captain was found guilty of unprofessional navigation two years later. The *Empire Brent* was repaired at the Alfred Dock at Birkenhead and, a month later, the Canadian war brides and their children rejoined her for an incident-free voyage to Halifax. My parents boarded her three years later unaware of this history. I wish I had found it for them before they died. My father always loved a good story. This little piece of the *Empire Brent's* history would no doubt have delighted him.

I have been in Liverpool now for almost seven years, and in that time I have travelled back to Sydney four times, and also to China, Vietnam, France Scotland, London, York, and to the old family haunts in Yorkshire. That is why I am here in Liverpool, in part at least, for the city's proximity to Yorkshire as a site of research; for getting to the heart of the matter about what my family was before it left and what it carried to Australia with it. Yorkshire – a ghost landscape inhabited by ghosts. Liverpool is my companion in this, a tolerant aunt of a city that is prepared to indulge my explorations. And so I wait, like an animal about to pounce. Waiting for the next story and the next, those narratives which, stitched together, make a person who they are and what they understand of themselves. Perhaps even what they'll leave behind one day when they travel between one place and the next, that hollowness where home and country should be located. As I write this, I am reminded of a sculpture. My thoughts have travelled to the statue called *I Viaggiatori* by the French artist, Bruno Catalano. It depicts a traveller and the empty core of him. Caroline, a close friend in Australia sent the image to me in one of those long, moody emails writers exchange when talking about ideas.

I'm not sure what matters to me most as I look at it; the statue itself or the friend in Australia I miss. This ambiguity is what makes Liverpool the ideal place from which to explore. It is a city with blurred edges, as though someone has taken to a charcoal sketch of the city, moistened their finger and rubbed.

It is a city with spaces to be filled.

Coda

Voices drift across the street. Music is playing on the stereo. The street voices rise and fall while Kathleen Ferrier sings 'Have you seen 'owt of my bonnie lad?' Melancholy. It is the perfect song for a mood of contemplation. My friends and I spoke of despair the other night. 'How would you define despair?' one asked. We each had a go. In the end, we discovered that despair comes with its own personal and individual characteristics, as unique as each of us.

I rang my brother today, hence my mood. He has been undergoing chemotherapy for cancer in the oesophagus. He, the little lad of Yorkshire, the long trip to Glasgow, the sea voyage, Hornby trains, and a new country. All of those things. He made a good life from a shy diffidence, bleak humour, left-wing politics, reflections on a past he was led away from as a boy. In Sydney, he made a new world eventually – a wife, three beautiful daughters, an inner well of generosity that meant he could never stay still: he just had to help everyone. Words from Henrik Ibsen's *Peer Gynt* always come to mind when I think of him:

That right hand in his pocket was the thing
That stamped his image sharply on our minds
And this strange shyness – this embarrassment
That would, on entering, always lag behind.

My brother has now reached a low point in his treatment caused by nausea, pain, tests and uncertainty. And despair. We talk over the miles, over the years, using a modern technology that overrides distance.

'What are you going to do when you are well again?' I ask.

He wants to buy a Harley Davidson motorbike, he says, an electric one, and take off to all the places he has never been.

'But you did that once on your old police Triumph,' I say. That bike was a recycled and restored police motor bike with a sidecar. We have a funny family photograph of my father acting the goat on it. My brother drove to Brisbane to visit our married cousin, the same cousin who as a little girl once wrote to our parents about the good life in Sydney.

'Only to Brisbane and back,' he says sadly, that little boy who sailed 12,000 miles. 'But I told the nurse I'll go for a long drive in the Lexus when I get home.'

'Go further,' I say, 'Broken Hill, Menindee Lakes, Narrabri, Moree. Drive to all the places you wish you'd been. Then come back here to England and stay with us for a while. We can explore Yorkshire together.'

'Mmnn,' he replies softly.

We both know this will not happen.

Kathleen Ferrier sings on. Those beautiful, mournful folk songs; we grew up on them. All my father's keening for Yorkshire. Irish songs, spirituals from the cotton pickers of America's south. Love songs. Paul Robeson or Richard Tauber, Enrico Caruso or Kenneth Mackellar singing of bonnie soldiers on the Christie's Music Hour. Kathleen Ferrier's voice, like Maria Callas', seems to carry a crack in it, a little, God-appeasing correction to perfection. Born in Lancashire, it is always a thrill to hear a hint of the North seep through a song by Brahms or Gluck or Schubert. Ferrier may have attended elocution lessons and voice training to ensure her pronunciation suited a woman with one of the finest contralto voices in the world, but I like to think there is something of her northern home there still, a secret code that only those from the north can detect. You can take the girl out of the North, as the saying goes, but you can't take the North out of the girl.

The COVID virus of 2020 brought home all that is awful about human distancing. During the virus-imposed period of isolation, social media acted as a conduit for the frustrations, sadness and boredom that resulted from being denied intimate contact with those you love. The virus cast us off into a new world, one in which a fear of contagion meant protecting oneself and those closest to us by staying apart for the sake of the frail elderly or those weakened already by illness. If I was in Sydney I still wouldn't be able to visit my immune-suppressed brother, I tell myself. We'd be contacting one another by Zoom or Teams or Skype from suburbs just a few kilometres apart, just as we have today over 12,000 electronic miles.

The pandemic's enforced interiority meant it was a time of sharing memories. Services like Facebook offered testament to the ways in which distance inevitably led us into stories, especially reflections about lost youth, past happy times, family activities. Images flourished on the site as people posted photos of themselves when they were young men and women of twenty; grainy pictures of parents alive or long-deceased, teasing Polaroids of social outings involving long-held friendships. Of particular poignancy was the fear that a parent, sibling or friend might get ill or die in isolation, alone, their death unheeded. This anxiety about an unaccompanied departure was one of the key narratives of the media's early coverage of the virus, asserting on daily news reports how profoundly important was every social ritual, especially those associated with death. By being with the dying, we shoulder some of the burden involved in their passing from one state of being to the next. Isolation meant the loved one's final journey would need to be taken alone.

As a child I watched how concerns about their families in England settled on my parents. First came news of my grandfather's death, then my aunt's. My parents' friends and colleagues got sick, some died. There was sadness when a beloved entertainer or politician in England died too, and being in Australia meant there was no sharing of the profound communal nostalgia and loss these deaths evoked. The tyranny of absence seemed most acute at these times, and I can only imagine now how distressing it was for my mother not to be able to attend her father's funeral. She never discussed this sorrow with us, but I felt it as I sat at the kitchen table the day she received the news of his death. While I drew a picture for school, she vented her grief quietly, despairingly, before my curious observation.

At these moments my parents' Northerness seemed to assert itself more potently than before. They had been making progress towards becoming more Australian through work, the house, the people they were getting to know in the neighbourhood and their community involvement with church and school, but each new sorrow drew them back to the past, to stories of lost times, and the regret that, even if they went back now, their past was lost to them. Their accents seemed to deepen in these times of crisis. The old vernacular and jokes seemed to tumble from their grief.

Migration narratives are full of these fears of distance and isolation – those backward glances as the shoreline recedes and fades. Departures are represented in paintings, plays, music and prose. Since the mid-eighteenth century, paintings have captured mass migrations including those of the Irish after the Great Famine or Scots after Highland enclosure. The art critic Robert O'Byrne is scathing about the sentimentality exhibited in Albert Grey's painting *The Emigrants' Last Farewell*. He calls it 'a spectacularly bad picture and not just because the artist was determined to squeeze every last drop of mawkishness out of the scene, with the young wife inevitably clutching a baby while attempting to staunch tears, her husband who sits on a basket carrying the couple's few possessions pluckily waving a hat at the rapidly vanishing shoreline.'

While O'Byrne saves his greatest criticism for the artist's lack of skill with his brush, his dismissal of the subject seems off mark. Anyone whose family has left one place sadly or regretfully or who has fled in haste, their life in danger, will have witnessed or heard about the brutal moment, one of acute realisation and loss, when the shape of a country and the family left behind fade into mist on the horizon. Like Lot's wife, they turn despite knowing it is best not to do so. At this point, this turning, I suspect migrants like my parents seize what they can and internalize it, in the process amplifying and distilling their former place, making it larger, stronger, more assertively part of themselves. Northern. We are of the North. Say it often, to yourselves and others: this is what makes you who you really are.

When the Brexit dealmaking was finally concluded on 31 December 2020, I felt doubly disconnected. I had taken for granted the freedom of movement my parents' Britishness had conferred upon me. I also had seen European citizenship as a reward for all those years we'd spent settling into our new Australian life. My EU passport was my prize for being British. My parents might have been working-class people from Yorkshire, we might have had our travails, but look at what my siblings and I had gained. As well as entry to Britain, my UK citizenship gave me the right to live and work in 27 other countries.

Freedom of movement has always been highly prized by the children of Australia's post-war years. Our parents' citizenship allowed us to apply for a passport from a place other than Australia. It set us off on our travels with a dual privilege, pursuing our cultural heritage, discovering new cultures. We backpacked, beach bummed and hitchhiked our way across the globe. It seems ironic that Australia's offshore detention centres were created by politicians who were the children of migrants, such as the Prime Ministers Tony Abbott and Julia Gillard, who had enjoyed the freedom to travel themselves. A kind of blindness seems to have set in, a heartlessness that involves a denial of one's own privilege in the face of other people's needs. The same situation occurs in the UK where a former Home Secretary, the child of Indian migrants fleeing from Idi Amin's Uganda to the UK, maintains a harsh line on migration and refuge despite her own family's dash to safety.

During Covid, fears about loss delivered their own credos about the importance of family and friends and how we relate to them. How we thrive around others. How our lives are enriched by daily conversations over a glass of wine or a cup of coffee. A virtual meeting just is not the same, especially when someone you love is dying. We need the tactile warmth of skin on skin. The virus, like numerous plagues and pandemics and wars before it, offered a common desire for life to be lived differently when all was safe again. We would live better, more kindly, more determined to make the most of our days and populate them with all the people we had missed. A resolve for improvements after crises like this must have underscored the desire for better things during and directly after the Second World War. How determined people were to get away from their lives in the shattered cities of Britain and Europe, to take flight to a new country, spurred on by a vision of a happier, freer life there, one to be lived in safety and prosperity. But in fleeing, millions – like the badly-crafted couple in Grey's painting – set forth in the full knowledge that they might never see their country and their loved ones again. Their journeys required courage and determination, and also an arrest of feeling. The future could be good, so long as the past that travelled with it was carefully recalibrated through cultural memory and a kind of generational hagiography. This word *hagiography* usually refers to the biography of someone famous whose reputation is preserved through the valedictory writings of an admirer or associate. In the case of migrants, the anthropomorphisation of place also creates a special engagement with its subject, a biography of a place so real, so missed, it's as close to you as a parent or grandparent. It lives and breathes in you.

England, and especially the north of the country, was my family's hagiographic subject. Yorkshire was a man in a tweed cloth cap, a woman with a feisty Sheffield accent, a Dalesman with his black-faced sheep, a group of Pennine ramblers admiring the Buttertub Pass as they ate a snap of bread and cheese. In my adolescence this portrait of a place expanded to include the characters in British new wave cinema; *Billy Liar, Loneliness of the Long-Distance Runner, Room at the Top, Kes*. These were cinematic representations of a place full of people who couldn't wait to escape, if not the place itself, then the class divisions manifest in smoking factory stacks, pit wheels and cobbled streets, or the back to backs and cramped rooms which defied anyone to dream of privacy.

Escape they did. Millions of them, and I am a child of this great, psychic upheaval. I hope this book reflects the mix of gratitude and wonder I feel, more and more potently as I grow old myself. What courage that voyage took and what personal costs were involved. As Stephanie Bishop wrote of her English grandmother:

> I started to understand the grief she had lived with for more than 40 years. This was partly because I, too, had come to feel attached to this place and could comprehend something of what she had lost. I then saw her in a completely different way: riven by opposing impulses, unsure of her own actions. I came to realise that my tendency to dismiss and overlook what, for my grandmother, amounted to an experience of exile, was part of a broader and persistent attitude towards this migrant group. The trials specific to British women migrants at that time were easily deemed insignificant. We generally resist describing migrants as exiles because it's assumed that the migrant is free to return. But after this conversation with my grandmother such a position seemed inaccurate, especially for this group of women, often with young children, and without independent means of their own that would allow them to choose otherwise.

I could only make sense of my parents' decision by experiencing the emotions involved in my own version of my family's migration – a return to England and all the triumphs and pain that entails. My quest then, is to live in the full comprehension of place. To reflect and write about the way it shaped who I am.

George Kouvaros gave voice to this need too. In *The Old Greeks*, he wrote:

> It is without doubt one of our great human frustrations that we learn life's lessons when it is too late to tell our

teachers that we have finally understood. The lessons I learned ... were not just about distance, then, but also about absence – an experience of absence that implicates our own place in the world.

For Andrea Cleland this type of reflection about family, place and the wider national experiences of migration represents 'a type of collective memory'. Family memory can mediate between national history and family history by keeping sites of memory alive. My family's history takes its place in both the personal and national narrative.

I talk to my dying brother across the miles. He doesn't like me to see how thin he's become, how bruised and grey like a washed-out old photo of the healthy man he once was, so sometimes to allow him the privacy he craves we talk with the camera off. He also has made me promise not to rush home to him. 'Just don't, OK?' he says in his bossy, big-brotherly way. 'I'll know I'm almost dead if you come home.' I promise to remember and write about him though, about his journey from Yorkshire to Sydney, from one kind of life to another, from potential to realisation. These memories, as well as informing this book, have sustained him through his punishing treatment and often added humour to the grimness of his condition. Looking back is enlivening when the future is fading.

We talk of that journey and what he remembers of it. How it changed him. How he grew up to be someone different in a different country. 'That took a lot of adjusting,' I say. He doesn't say much to that, then, 'life is all about adjustment, isn't it?' Courage too, I say. And sharing stories. And being there even if just in spirit. It is recognizing also that people make sacrifices and we often don't realise this until it is too late to thank them.

My brother died a few days after that conversation. And so, to my parents and siblings I can now say this: I salute your courage and vision. I appreciate what you did for the family. I now understand.

Acknowledgements

My thanks to my partner John Daniels for his ongoing love and support. Thanks also to my family who provided me with so many photographs and memories. To my brother's partner, Lyn and his three daughters, April, Alison and Amanda. Thanks also to my colleagues in our nonfiction group at Liverpool John Moores University – Kate Walchester, Helen Tookey, Jude Piesse, Jamie Whitehead, Joe Moran and Jo Price. The Liverpool Maritime and Slavery Museum was very helpful with archives. Thanks also to Liverpool John Moores university for a small grant to follow in my parents' footsteps to Sheffield, Barnsley, Royston and the Glasgow docks.

It is no longer possible to thank my brother, Brian, but he was a supportive and engaged presence all through the writing of this memoir, despite the pain he was experiencing. It has been of particular importance to me to share his story in this way and to celebrate his journey.

Chapter References

INTRODUCTION

Wood, James, *On Not Going Home,* London Review of Books, Vol.36, No. 4, February 2014

Wood, as above

Kouvaros, George, *The Old Greeks*, New South Books, Sydney, 2018, p.129

Weil, Simone, *The Need for Roots*, 1943, Routledge, London, 1952, trans. Arthur Wills, p.41

Darian-Smith, Kate and Hamilton, Paula, *Remembering Migration: Oral Histories and Heritage in Australia*, Palgrave Macmillan, Sydney, 2019, p.6

Gusdorf, George, *Speaking*, North Western University Press, Illinois, 1965, p. 268

Atef Abu Saif, https://www.theguardian.com/commentis free/2018/may/14/palestinians-israel-nakba-day-gazans, 14 May, 2018

CHAPTER 1. THE SEA

Hammerton and Thomson, *Ten Pound Poms: Australia's Invisible Migrants*, Manchester University Press, Manchester, 2005, p.62

Whitlock in Darian-Smith and Hamilton, *Remembering Migration: Oral Histories and Migration in Australia* p.9, as above

Clare, Horatio, *Down to the Sea in Ships,* Chatto and Windus, London, 2014, p. 10

Kouvaros, as above

Atef Abu Saif, as above

Said, Edward, *Reflection on Exile and Other Essays*, Harvard University Press, Cambridge, MA, 2001, p.4

Haghe, Ghassan, 'Migration, Food, Memory, and Home-Building' in *Memory: Histories, Theories, Debates*, Editor(s): Sussanah Radstone and Bill Schwartz, Fordham University Press, p.416-417

Said, as above, p. 4

Radstone in Darian-Smith and Hamilton p. 240, as above

Freeman as above, p.272

Bishop, Stephanie, My grandmother's £10 'exile' returned to haunt me | Family | The Guardian, 17 September, 2016

Hammerton and Thomson, as above, p. 42.

Baucom, Ian, 'Mournful Histories: Narratives of Post Imperial Melancholy', Modern Fiction Studies, 42.2 (1996) p. 271

Hammerton and Thomson, as above, p.9

Bannon in Hammerton and Thomson, as above

Kouvaros, as above, p. 192

Kouvaros, as above, p. 19

Chapter 2. Migrants from the North

Gide, Andre, *The Counterfeiters*, Penguin Classics, London, 1996

Darien-Smith and Hamilton, p. 9

Hammerton and Thomson. p. 325

Kapllani, Gazmed, *A Short Border Handbook*, Portobello Books, 2013, p.10

Hammerton and Thomson, as above, p. 279

Hammerton and Thomson, p.35

Lewitt *No Snow in December*, William Heineman, Melbourne, 1986

Nicholson, Paul, *Occupational Medicine*, Volume 68, Issue 6, August 2018, Pages 352–35

Haghe as above p.417

Auge, Marc, *Oblivion*, Univ of Minnesota Press, 2004, p.17

Blanco, Caicedo and Loranzo, SBS online, 14/9/2020

Sontag, Susan, *On Photography*, Penguin, New York, 1979

Kouvaros, George, as above, p. 59

Blanco, Caicedo and Loranzo, SBS online, 14/9/2020

Tolstoy, Leo, *Anna Karenina*, p. 2

Lents, Nathan, 'The Meaning and Meaninglessness of Genealogy' https://www.psychologytoday.com/gb/blog/beastly-behavior/201801/the-meaning-and-meaninglessness-genealogy

Barthes, Roland, *Autobiography*, Polity Press, 2016

Kouvaros, George, p. 182

Maconie, Stuart, *Pies and Prejudice: In search of the North*, Ebury Press, 2008, p.31

Maconie, as above, p. 33

Woods, as above, p. 8

Hemon, Aleksander, 'Bread is Practically Sacred': How the Taste of Home sustained my refugee parents, The Guardian, 13 June, 2019) https://www.theguardian.com/food/2019/jun/13/bread-is-practically-sacred-how-the-taste-of-home-sustained-my-refugee-parents

Hammerton and Thomson, as above, p. 350

Said, Edward, as above, p. 143

Wainwright, Martin, *True North*, Guardian Books, UK, p.52

Wainwright, as above, p. 52

Hammerton and Thomson, as above, p. 273

Hage, as above, pp.426/427

Baucom, as above, p. 273

Wood, James, as above pp 5/8

Chapter 3. Home

Hammerton and Thomson, as above, p.226

Bethell, https://www.bbc.co.uk/wales/arts/yourvideo/media/pages/val_bethell_01.shtml, BBC, 2003

Hepworth, Shelley, 'The Smell of Gum Trees and Rejection: the Australians locked out of 'home' by Covid Border Closures', The Guardian, 27 March, 2022

Wood, as above, p.8

Angelou, Maya, *Rainbow in the Cloud: The Wisdom of Maya Angelou*, Random House, New York, 2014, p. 5

Radstone in Darian-Smith and Hamilton, p. 255

Bachelard, *The Poetics of Space*, p. 6

Bachelard, as above, p. 6

Eliot, TS, *The Family Reunion*, Faber, London, 1966

Roberts, Carol, Fibro Homes Made Home Ownership Attainable after the War, *The Hawkesbury Gazette,* November 27, 2015, https://www.hawkesburygazette.com.au/story/3522825/history-when-fibro-meant-dream-home/

Hammerton and Thomson, as above, p. 12

Pullan, Nicola, *Just a Roof Over Their Heads: Temporary Dwellings on Sydney's Urban Fringe 1945 to 1960*, p.239

Haghe, p.419

Kouvaros, as above, p. 59

Naipaul in Baucom, as above, p.259

Bachelard, *The Poetics of Space*, p.6

Balakjian Aram, in Paula Cocozza, 'A Window to the Past': how old photos brought my parents' empty house back to life', The Guardian, 2 August, 2019

Kinkenborg, The Smithsonian Magazine, May, 2012

Balakjian in Cocozza, as above.

Hepworth, Shelley, 'The Smell of Gum Trees and Rejection: the Australians locked out of 'home' by Covid Border Closures', The Guardian, 27 March, 2022

Davis, Rhett, 'Avoiding it: Writing fiction about place without writing about it', Text, Vol 24, April 2020

Darian-Smith and Hamilton, as above, p.2

Falkener, Suzanne. Randolph Stow's farewell to Australia for a life of self-exile (smh.com.au) Sydney Morning Herald, 2 February, 2016, Sydney

Stowe, To Fix the Identity of a Raw Democracy, Address to the Fellowship of Australian Writers, 1973

Randstone as above, p. 253

Leong, Hou, http://press-files.anu.edu.au/downloads/press /p14881/html/ch07s03.html

Virendranath, SBS Radio, 29/1/2018

Sahlins, *Boundaries: The Making of France and Spain in the Pyrenees*, University of California Press, 1989, p. 525.

Niven, Alex, 'Why it's time to Stop Talking about English Identity', The Guardian 15 July, 2020

Wills, Sarah and Darian-Smith, Kate, 'Beefeaters, Bobbies, and a New Varangian Guard? Negotiating Forms of "Britishness" in Suburban Australia', p.2

Hammerton and Thomson, as above, pp. 133–4

Loan, *New Humans of Australia*, https://aussiestories.org/

Cleland, Andrea, in Darian-Smith, Kate and Hamilton, Paula, *Migration: Oral Histories and Heritage in Australia*, Palgrave Macmillan, Sydney, 2019, p.157

Hammerton and Thomson, as above, p. 239

Singer, Ivan Bashevis, *The Slave*, Penguin Modern Classics, London, 2012, p.8

Hammerton and Thomson, as above, p. 356

Fotis Kapetopoulos https://neoskosmos.com/en/152350/to-be-a-wog-or-not-to-be/ 2019

Rachwani, Mostafa, 'I didn't want to be a 'Lebo' growing up in Australia, but I came to love who I am' The Guardian, Tuesday 5 January, 2021

Rachwani, as above

Berger, John, 'Ev'ry Time We Say Goodbye', *Selected Essays of John Berger*, Pantheon, 2001

Murrat et al in Stephens, SMH 2003

Chapter 5. Return

Wood, James, as above, p. 6

Kouvaros, George, as above, p.130

Hammerton and Thomson, p.273

Clare, Horatio, as above, pp. 10-11

Davis, Rhett, 'Avoiding it: Writing fiction about place without writing about it', Text, Vol 24, April 2020

Kouvaros, p. 120

Baucom, as above, p. 141

Schwartz, Oscar, 'On Leaving a City', (https://oscar-schwartz.substack.com/p/on-leaving-a-city)

Bryson, Bill, *The Road to Little Dribbling*, Doubleday, London, 2015, p.346

Chapter 6. Liverpool

Swerdlow, Michael in Stuart Maconie's book, *Pies and Prejudice*, p. 63

Young, Jeff, *Ghost Town*, Little Toller, 2020, p. 10

Johnson, Boris, in Maconie, as above, p. 64

Henshaw in Maconie, as above, p. 68

Young, Jeff, *Ghost Town*, as above, p. 85

Hammerton and Thomson, p.22
Gatrells Peter, The Unsettling of Europe, Allen Lane, 2020
Ibsen, Henrik, *Peer Gynt*, Act V
O'Byrne, Robert, Apollo Magazine 11/12/13, A Sentimental Lot: The Emigrants' Last Farewell by Alfred Grey | Apollo Magazine (apollo-magazine.com)
Bishop, Stephanie, as above
Kouvaros, George, as above, p. 188

Bibliography

Atef Abu Saif, https://www.theguardian.com/commentis-free/2018/may/14/palestinians-israel-nakba-day-gazans, 14 May, 2018
Auge, Marc, *Oblivion*, Univ of Minnesota Press, 2004
Bachelard, *The Poetics of Space*, Penguin books, New York, 2014
Balakjian Aram, in Paula Cocozza, 'A Window to the Past': how old photos brought my parents' empty house back to life', The Guardian, 2 August, 2019
Bannon in Hammerton and Thomson, *Ten Pound Poms: Australia's Invisible Migrants*, Manchester University Press, Manchester, 2005
Barthes, Roland, *Autobiography*, Polity Press, Cambridge, 2016
Baucom, Ian, 'Mournful Histories: Narratives of Post Imperial Melancholy', Modern Fiction Studies, 42.2 (1996)
Berger, John, 'Ev'ry Time We Say Goodbye', Selected Essays of John Berger, Pantheon, 2001

Bethell, https://www.bbc.co.uk/wales/arts/yourvideo/media/pages/val_bethell_01.shtml, BBC, 2003

Bishop, Stephanie, My grandmother's £10 'exile' returned to haunt me | Family | The Guardian

Blanco, Caicedo and Loranzo, SBS online, 14/9/2020, https://www.sbs.com.au/language/spanish/es/article/the-untold-story-of-the-sbs-broadcaster-who-died-on-9-11/whk98wynf

Bryson, Bill, *The Road to Little Dribbling*, Doubleday, London, 2015

Clare, Horatio, *Down to the Sea in Ships,* Chatto and Windus, London, 2014

Cleland, Andrea, in Darian-Smith, Kate and Hamilton, Paula, *Migration: Oral Histories and Heritage in Australia*, Palgrave Macmillan, Sydney, 2019

Darian-Smith, Kate and Hamilton, Paula, *Remembering Migration: Oral Histories and Heritage in Australia*, Palgrave Macmillan, Sydney, 2019

Davis, Rhett, 'Avoiding it: Writing fiction about place without writing about it', Text, Vol 24, April 2020

Eliot, TS, *The Family Reunion*, Faber, London, 1966

Falkener, Suzanne. Randolph Stow's farewell to Australia for a life of self-exile (smh.com.au) Sydney Morning Herald, 2 February, 2016, Sydney

Gatrells, Peter, *The Unsettling of Europe: The Great Migration 1945 to the present,* Allen Lane, 2020

Gide, Andre, *The Counterfeiters*, Penguin Classics, London, 1996

Gusdorf, George, *Speaking*, North Western University Press, Evanston, IL, 1965

Haghe, Ghassan, 'Migration, Food, Memory, and Home-Building' in Memory: Histories, Theories, Debates, Editor(s): Susannah Radstone and Bill Schwarz,

Fordham University Press, 2010

Hammerton and Thomson, *Ten Pound Poms: Australia's Invisible Migrants*, Manchester University Press, Manchester, 2005

Hemon, Aleksander, 'Bread is Practically Sacred': How the Taste of Home sustained my refugee parents, The Guardian, 13 June, 2019) https://www.theguardian.com/food/2019/jun/13/bread-is-practically-sacred-how-the-taste-of-home-sustained-my-refugee-parents

Hepworth, Shelley, 'The Smell of Gum Trees and Rejection: the Australians locked out of 'home' by Covid Border Closures', The Guardian, 27 March, 2022

Ibsen, Henrik, *Peer Gynt and Brand*, Penguin Classics, London, 2016

Johnson, Boris, in Maconie, Stuart, *Pies and Prejudice: In search of the North*, Ebury Press, London, 2008

Kapllani, Gazmed, *A Short Border Handbook*, Portobello Books, London, 2013

Fotis Kapetopoulos https://neoskosmos.com/en/152350/to-be-a-wog-or-not-to-be/ 2019

Kinkenborg, The Smithsonian Magazine, May, 2012

Kouvaros, George, *The Old Greeks*, New South Books, Sydney, 2018

Lents, Nathan, 'The Meaning and Meaninglessness of Genealogy' https://www.psychologytoday.com/gb/blog/beastly-behavior/201801/the-meaning-and-meaninglessness-genealogy

Leong, Hou, (http://press-files.anu.edu.au/downloads/press/p14881/html/cho7so3.html

Lewitt *No Snow in December*, William Heineman, Melbourne, 1986

Loan, *New Humans of Australia*: https://aussiestories.org/

Maconie, Stuart, *Pies and Prejudice: In search of the North*,

Ebury Press, London, 2008

Nicholson, Paul, *Occupational Medicine*, Volume 68, Issue 6, August 2018, Pages 352–35

Niven, Alex, 'Why it's time to Stop Talking about English Identity', The Guardian 15 July, 2020

O'Byrne, Robert, 'A Sentimental Lot', Apollo Magazine 11/12/13, A Sentimental Lot: The Emigrants' Last Farewell by Alfred Grey | Apollo Magazine (apollo-magazine.com)

Pullan, Nicola, *Just a Roof Over Their Heads: Temporary Dwellings on Sydney's Urban Fringe 1945 to 1960*, Temporary Dwellings on Sydney's Urban Fringe 1945 to 1960 – DocsLib

Rachwani, Mostafa, 'I didn't want to be a 'Lebo' growing up in Australia, but I came to love who I am' The Guardian, Tuesday 5 January, 2021

Radstone in Darian-Smith and Hamilton, Darian-Smith, Kate and Hamilton, Paula, *Migration: Oral Histories and Heritage in Australia*, Palgrave Macmillan, Sydney, 2019

Roberts, Carol, *The Hawkesbury Gazette*

Said, Edward, *Reflection on Exile and Other Essays*, Harvard University Press, 2001

Sahlins, *Boundaries: The Making of France and Spain in the Pyrenees*, University of California Press, 1989

Schwartz, Oscar, 'On Leaving a City', (https://oscar-schwartz.substack.com/p/on-leaving-a-city)

Singer, Ivan Bashevis, *The Slave*, Penguin Modern Classics, London, 2012

Sontag, Susan, *On Photography*, Penguin, New York, 1979

Stowe, *To Fix the Identity of a Raw Democracy*, 1973

Swerdlow, Michael in Maconie, Stuart, *Pies and Prejudice: In search of the North*, Ebury Press, London, 2008p. 63

Tolstoy, Leo, *Anna Karenina*, Wordsworth Classics, 1990

Virendranath, SBS Radio, https://www.sbs.com.au/language/nitv-radio/en, 29/1/2018

Wainwright, Martin, *True North*, Guardian Books, London, 2012

Weil, Simone, *The Need for Roots*, 1943, Routledge, London, 1952, trans. Arthur Wills

Whitlock in Darian-Smith and Hamilton, *Remembering Migration: Oral Histories and Migration in Australia*

Wills, Sarah and Darian-Smith, Kate, 'Beefeaters, Bobbies, and a New Varangian Guard? Negotiating Forms of "Britishness" in Suburban Australia', History of Intellectual Culture, Vol 4, No. 1, 2004

Wood, James, *On Not Going Home,* London Review of Books, Vol.36, No. 4, February 2014

Young, Jeff, *Ghost Town*, Little Toller, Dorset, UK, 2020